URNAL OF
RATE
CITIZENSHIP
Issue 64
December 2016

Theme Issue: **The United Nations Global Compact and the Encyclical Laudato Si**

Guest Editor:
Oliver F. Williams, University of Notre Dame, USA

print ISSN 1470-5001   *online* ISSN 2051-4700

THE JOURNAL OF CORPORATE CITIZENSHIP

General Editor David F. Murphy, Institute for Leadership and Sustainability (IFLAS), University of Cumbria, UK
Regional Editor *North America*: Professor Sandra Waddock, Boston College, Carroll School of Management, USA
Managing Editor Benjamin Kata Finau, The University of Auckland, New Zealand
Publisher Victoria Halliday, Greenleaf Publishing, UK
Assistant Publisher Anna Kemball, Greenleaf Publishing, UK
Production Editor Chris Maher, Greenleaf Publishing, UK

CORRESPONDENCE

The Journal of Corporate Citizenship encourages response from its readers to any of the issues raised in the journal. All correspondence is welcomed and should be sent to the General Editor c/o Greenleaf Publishing, Salts Mill, Victoria Road, Saltaire, BD18 3LA, UK; jcc@greenleaf-publishing.com.

All content should be submitted via **online submission**. For more information see the journal homepage at www.greenleaf-publishing.com/jcc.

Books to be considered for review should be marked for the attention of the Book Review Editor c/o Greenleaf Publishing, Salts Mill, Victoria Road, Saltaire, BD18 3LA, UK; jcc@greenleaf-publishing.com.

• All articles published in *The Journal of Corporate Citizenship* are assessed by an external panel of business professionals, consultants and academics.

• *The Journal of Corporate Citizenship* is indexed with and included in: **Cabells, EBSCO,** the **Association of Business Schools Academic Journal Guide, ABDC** and **Journalseek.net**. It is monitored by "Political Science and Government Abstracts" and "Sociological Abstracts".

SUBSCRIPTION RATES

The Journal of Corporate Citizenship is a quarterly journal, appearing in March, June, September and December of each year. Cheques should be made payable to Greenleaf Publishing and sent to the address below.

Annual online subscription
Individuals: £80.00/€112.50/US$150.00
Organizations: £540.00/€650.00/US$850.00

Annual print and online subscription
Individuals: £90.00/€120.00/US$160.00
Organizations: £550.00/€672.50/US$860.00

Annual print subscription
Individuals: £80.00/€112.50/US$150.00
Organizations: £180.00/€240.00/US$320.00

The Journal of Corporate Citizenship
Greenleaf Publishing Ltd, Aizlewood Business Centre, Aizlewood's Mill, Nursery Street, Sheffield S3 8GG, UK
Tel: +44 (0)114 282 3475   Fax: +44 (0)114 282 3476   Email: jcc@greenleaf-publishing.com.
Or order from our website: www.greenleaf-publishing.com/journals/journal-of-corporate-citizenship.

ADVERTISING

The Journal of Corporate Citizenship will accept a strictly limited amount of display advertising in future issues. It is also possible to book inserts. Suitable material for promotion includes publications, conferences and consulting services. For details on rates and availability, please email jcc@greenleaf-publishing.com.

FSC
www.fsc.org
MIX
Paper from
responsible sources
FSC® C013604

Printed in the UK on environmentally friendly, acid-free paper from managed forests by CPI Group (UK) Ltd, Croydon

DOI: [10.9774/GLEAF.4700.2016.de.00002]

Editorial

Issue 64 *December 2016*

David F. Murphy

Institute for Leadership and Sustainability (IFLAS), University of Cumbria, UK

The Journal of Corporate Citizenship (JCC) Issue 64 is a Special Issue on "The UN Global Compact and the Encyclical Laudato Si", guest-edited by Oliver Williams, C.S.C., Director of the Center for Ethics and Religious Values in Business, Mendoza College of Business, University of Notre Dame. In collaboration with the United Nations Global Compact Office, the University of Notre Dame hosted a conference in April 2016—"A Global Compact for Sustainable Development: Advancing Care for Our Common Home"—to discuss the *Encyclical Laudato Si* and the UN Sustainable Development Goals (SDGs). In his Guest Editorial, Williams highlights the major contributions of each of the articles in this issue that arose from that conference.

JCC 64 is not the first issue of the journal with a UN Global Compact focus. In the Autumn of 2003, I co-edited *JCC* 11 which was a theme issue on "The United Nations Global Compact". In our Introduction to the issue, fellow guest editors Malcolm McIntosh, Rupesh Shah and I acknowledged that the Compact was in its infancy and that the articles in *JCC* 11 were "tentative and exploratory", as was the initiative itself at the time. And in her Editorial, then General Editor Sandra Waddock noted that early

> reactions in the public arena ... ranged from kudos for using the UN's moral authority and convening power to push business into principled and responsible actions with respect to human rights, labour and the natural environment, to charges of corporate "bluewashing" (wrapping company actions in the blue UN flag without real substance behind them) (p. 3).

Waddock concluded then that "the truth ... probably lies somewhere in between"(p. 3).

Before looking forward, let us look back at the evolution of the Global Compact from its inception to the present day. In January 1999, the seventh UN Secretary-General, Kofi Annan, first invited the international business community to enter into a global compact with the UN and civil society, and "articulated a vision of a more sustainable and just world with partnership as its cornerstone" (Murphy, 2002, p. 63). But, even as the Global Compact was still emerging at the turn of the century, the idea of UN–business collaboration was under attack. Corporate watchdogs such as the Transnational Resource & Action Center challenged the Secretary-General, participating UN agencies and their new corporate partners from the Compact's outset (Karliner, Cavanaugh and Bennis, 1999; Transnational Resource & Action Center, 2000). Global Compact critique and challenge from civil society, academia and from within the UN system itself has continued over the years (see: Richter, 2004; Knight & Smith, 2008; Utting & Zammit, 2009). Nonetheless, 16 years on, the Global Compact claims to be the world's largest corporate sustainability initiative with its website listing more than 11,000 participants, comprising approximately 9,000 business entities and 2,000 other organizations.

In recent years, the Global Compact and other corporate sustainability, corporate citizenship and corporate social responsibility (CSR) initiatives have continued to face scrutiny from civil society and other sectors. In the late 1990s, the primary social and environmental critics of large corporates were NGOs, trade unions and anti-globalization activist groups. With the publication of *Laudato Si* in May 2015, the Roman Catholic Church and its leaders are presenting new challenges to globalization and some of its key international players such as corporations, governments and the UN system. For example, note this 2015 critical analysis of the global economic system by Cardinal Peter Turkson of Ghana, President of the Pontifical Council for Justice & Peace and recently appointed by Pope Francis as the first prefect of the Dicastery for the Promotion of Integral Human Development: "Much of world remains in poverty, despite abundant resources, while a privileged global elite controls the bulk of the world's wealth and consumes the bulk of its resources" (see Kirchgaessner, 2015). And this overt corporate critique from *Laudato Si* itself: "the social and environmental responsibility of businesses often gets reduced to a series of marketing and image-enhancing measures" (p. 142).

Cardinal Turkson's words and the excerpt from *Laudato Si* cited above would not have been out of place in an activist critique of global business in 1999 or more recently. Even Georg Kell (2016), the Global Compact's Founding Director, has recently voiced his concern about "tangential and ultimately unsustainable philanthropic contributions" which are characteristic of many CSR programmes. Kell's new agenda for global corporations is "to adopt a bolder, more activist approach to address the challenges to continued prosperity" founded on "corporate statesmanship, which emphasizes collective leadership and not just responsible individual participation". The current Executive Director of the Global Compact, Lise Kingo (2015), agrees with her predecessor and offers an effective bridge to the Guest Editorial and articles that follow in this Special Issue:

> Whether we are talking about scaling up action on the Guiding Principles [on business and human rights] or contributing to the SDGs, we need leadership. Businesses must have top-level commitment and accountability to assess their impacts, engage in genuine dialogue with rights-holders, and to innovate their business models (p. 3).

Laudato Si is hopeful: "Business is a noble vocation, directed to pursuing wealth and improving our world"

(p. 129). The essays that follow offer a path to guide that hope.

References

Karliner, J., Cavanaugh, J. & Bennis, P. (1999). *A Perilous Partnership: The United Nation Development Programme's Flirtation with Corporate Collaboration.* San Francisco: Transnational Resource & Action Center in collaboration with the Institute for Policy Studies and the Council on International and Public Affairs. Retrieved from: http://s3.amazonaws.com/corpwatch.org/downloads/perilous.pdf

Kell, G. (2016, October 4). From Corporate Citizenship to Corporate Statesmanship, LinkedIn posting. Retrieved from: https://www.linkedin.com/pulse/from-corporate-citizenship-statesmanship-georg-kell

Kingo, L. (2015, November 18, 16:40). Remarks of Ms. Lise Kingo, Executive Director of UN Global Compact United Nations Forum on Business and Human Rights. Geneva. Retrieved from: http://www.ohchr.org/Documents/Issues/Business/ForumSession4/LiseKingo_remarks.pdf

Kirchgaessner, S. (2015, April 28). Vatican official calls for moral awakening on global warming. *The Guardian.* Retrieved from: https://www.theguardian.com/environment/2015/apr/28/vatican-climate-change-summit-to-highlight-moral-duty-for-action

Knight, G. & Smith, J. (2008). The Global Compact and Its Critics: Activism, Power Relations, and Corporate Social Responsibility. In Leatherman, J. (Ed.), *Discipline and Punishment in Global Politics* (pp. 191-214). London: Palgrave Macmillan.

Murphy, D.F. (2002). Towards a Global Compact Agenda for African Enterprises. In Chatterjee, L. (Ed.), *Words into Action* (pp. 63-67). London: Faircourt and International Institute for Environment and Development (IIED). Retrieved from: http://pubs.iied.org/pdfs/9191IIED.pdf

Pope Francis I (2015, May 24). *Encyclical Letter "Laudato Si" of The Holy Father Francis on Care for Our Common Home.* Libreria Editrice Vaticana, Given in Rome at Saint Peter's. Retrieved from: https://laudatosi.com/

Richter, J. (2004). *Public–Private Partnerships and International Health Policy-Making. How Can Public Interests Be Safeguarded?* Helsinki: Development Policy Information Unit, Ministry for Foreign Affairs of Finland.

Transnational Resource & Action Center (2000). *Tangled Up in Blue: Corporate Partnerships at the United Nations.* San Francisco: Transnational Resource & Action Center (TRAC). Retrieved from: http://s3.amazonaws.com/corpwatch.org/downloads/tangled.pdf

Utting, P. & Zammit, A. (2009). United Nations–Business Partnerships: Good Intentions and Contradictory Agendas. *Journal of Business Ethics.* 90:39-56. doi:10.1007/s10551-008-9917-7.

Waddock, S. (2003). Editorial. *Journal of Corporate Citizenship* 11 (September): 3-4.

DOI: [10.9774/GLEAF.4700.2016.de.00003]

Guest Editorial

Adapting to and Expanding the Social Expectations on Business

The Common Theme in Laudato Si and the UN Sustainable Development Goals

Oliver F. Williams

University of Notre Dame, USA

- Social licence to operate
- Social contract
- Sustainable Development Goals
- Laudato Si
- United Nations Global Compact
- Purpose of business

In April 2016 the Center for Ethics and Religious Values in Business of the Mendoza College of Business at the University of Notre Dame with the United Nations Global Compact (UNGC)Office convened a group of scholars and business leaders to discuss the Encyclical Laudato Si (LS) and the UN Sustainable Development Goals (SDGs). The articles in this special issue are from that conference; the hope is that they will provoke your thinking and lead to new action to make the world a better place. This editorial offers an interpretation of how the SDGs and LS might influence scholars and business leaders and it also provides a context for the articles that follow.

Oliver Williams is a member of the faculty of the Mendoza College of Business at the University of Notre Dame and is the Director of the Center for Ethics and Religious Values in Business. Williams is the editor or author of 20 books as well as numerous articles on business ethics in journals such as the *Harvard Business Review, California Management Review, Business Ethics Quarterly, Journal of Business Ethics, Journal of Corporate Citizenship,* and *Theology Today. Recent books include Corporate Social Responsibility: The Role of Business in Sustainable Development and Sustainable Development: The UN Millennium Development Goals, The UN Global Compact and The Common Good* (Editor), both published in 2014. He served as Associate Provost of the University of Notre Dame from 1987 to 1994 and is a past Chair of the Social Issues Division of the Academy of Management. In 2006, he was appointed a member of the three-person Board of Directors at the United Nations Global Compact Foundation. The United Nations Global Compact is the world's largest voluntary corporate citizenship initiative with over 9,000 businesses in 168 countries as members. For the last 15 years, from May until July, Williams served as a Visiting Professor at theGraduate School of Business of the University of Cape Town and Stellenbosch University. He has also served as the Donald Gordon Visiting Fellow at the University of Cape Town. In the 2012–13 academic year, he served as an International Scholar at Kyung Hee University in Seoul, South Korea and has taught there during the month of July since 2000. He also has been named as Professor Extraordinary at the University of Stellenbosch in South Africa. Williams is an ordained Catholic priest in the Congregation of Holy Cross.

Mendoza College of Business
University of Notre Dame
Notre Dame, Indiana 46556

oliver.f.williams.80@nd.edu

S THE CALL FOR BUSINESS to take on projects that are designed to alleviate global poverty and enhance the environment based on a business case or a moral case? Will these projects earn more money for a company (the business case) or should they be done simply because they are the right thing to do (the moral case) (Vogel, 2005; Gates, 2008)? I argue that the moral case is slowly transforming into a key element of the business case and that this transformation is driven by the changing expectations that global consumers have for business. Today consumers have much greater expectations for the role that business should play in meeting social and environmental issues (Zadek, 2004; Mattenand Moon, 2008; Porter and Kramer, 2011). To be sure, no one is arguing that business should assume the role of government but there is a case to be made that business should meet some of these expectations and that this is a key requirement in securing and maintaining social acceptance and public trust, what is sometimes called a company's social licence to operate (Haufler, 2001; Gunningham *et al.*, 2004; Nelsen, 2006; Burke *et al.*, 2011; Prno *et al.*, 2012).

It should be clear that the universal values of the principles of the Global Compact (Williams, 2004) and the Sustainable Development Goals (SDGs) fit naturally with the way business ethics is taught at Notre Dame and other business schools. Business ethics at Notre Dame is asking *normative* questions not simply *descriptive* questions. For example, the question moves beyond, "Do people believe that a company should pay the lowest wages possible?" the descriptive question, to the normative question: "Should a company pay the lowest wages possible?" And, if not, why not? Rather than simply providing a descriptive characterization of people's beliefs, the common effort in developing the SDGs lays the groundwork for developing reasonable normative claims largely based on human rights and justice (Donaldson, 1989; Velasquez, 2015). Other issues such as those from labour, the environment and corruption are the focus of the ten principles of the United Nations Global Compact (UNGC) (Williams, 2014a). That being said, the attempt to bring ethical behaviour in business to scale is a work in progress. One way to view the common theme in the SDGs and the encyclical Laudato Si is that both of these endeavours are charting the way forward for a new social contract (Donaldson, 1982; Donaldson and Dunfee, 1994), reformulating the terms of the social licence to operate so that business itself is part of the contract. Business is asked to advance the global goals championed in the SDGs and the encyclical; that is, overcoming global poverty and enhancing sustainability (Williams, 2014c).

The moral and political foundations of the state advanced by the political philosophers of the Enlightenment, John Locke, Jean-Jacques Rousseau and Thomas Hobbes, were formulated in terms of the "social contract", a concept dating from the Greek Sophists and other ancient philosophers. Here political legitimacy was given to a government that met the social expectations for security, mutual protection and welfare. The implied social contract with businesses, until relatively recently, was that they should see their primary duty as providing good products at a fair price while following the prevailing ethical customs. The SDGs and the encyclical Laudato Si are a call to expand the social expectations on business. Many scholars and activists have been arguing that with the huge aggregates of money, management skills and power under the control of multinational businesses, these organizations do have moral obligations to assume some responsibility for poverty and care for the global community. This represents a major change in the social contract with business and, as the title of the UN programme, the Global Compact, suggests, this change is increasingly recognized (Paine, 2003; Frederick, 2006; Mackey and Sisodia, 2013).

Thus one of the key drivers for an expansion of what constitutes "responsible business conduct" today is social expectations. This is highlighted by the use of the term in recent UN documents on human rights: the UN "Protect, Respect and Remedy" Framework (UN, 2008) and the UN Guiding Principles on Business and Human Rights (UN, 2011). Here there is a clear connection between economic and social risks (Cragg, 2012; Ruggie, 2014). "Whereas governments define the scope of legal compliance, the broader scope of the responsibility to respect is defined by social expectations—as part of what is sometimes called a company's social license to operate" (UN, 2008, para 54).

It should be clear, however, that the need for business to meet public expectations as a part of the social licence to operate is not a new idea. Frank Abrams, an executive in what is now called Exxon, as chairman of the board of directors, wrote in a 1951 article in the *Harvard Business Review* a clarion call that is now increasingly recognized. "Public approval is no less essential to the continued existence of today's kind of business than adequate capital, or efficient management" (Abrams, 1951, p. 30).

In 1960, Keith Davis, a pioneer in the field of corporate social responsibility, formulated what he called the Iron Law of Responsibility (Davis, 1960). Where there is power, there is also responsibility and, according to Davis, if a business does not use its power in a way that society considers responsible, it will lose that power. To be perceived as legitimate by society, a company must do more than produce good products at a fair price while following the law and ethical customs. That social contract is being replaced by a new one and the SDGs and Laudato Si are an attempt to set the terms of the new social contract. If these documents can persuade the public of the necessity for action, business will meet these expectations. This represents a changing social contract between business and society.

The key challenge for business leaders today is to narrow the gap between the values of business and those of society (Carroll, 1999; Palazzo andScherer, 2006). Business is most interested in tracking the values of society. A 1999 poll by Environics International (now called GlobeScan International) questioned 25,000 people in 23 countries about corporate social responsibility. Called The Millennium Poll on Corporate Social Responsibility, the survey found that two-thirds of the respondents wanted companies to go beyond the traditional roles (make profit, pay taxes, create jobs and obey all laws) and assume a broader role (set higher ethical standards and help build a better society) (GlobeScan, 1999). As these moral issues, advancing ethics and building a better society, are subsumed into social expectations for business, they become part of the social licence to operate and thus key elements of the business case. For if there is a significant gap between what a business is doing and what the public expects, there is public pressure for additional regulations and legislation entailing what economists call "transaction costs" (Fukuyama, 1995; Mayer *et al.*, 1995). Consider the change in the terms of the social licence to operate and the new transaction costs for business involved with the 2002 US Sarbanes-Oxley law enacted after Enron and the other accounting scandals. Auditing expenses have increased 200 to 300% as a result of that legislation. A similar finding is evident when analysing the 2010 Dodd-Frank Wall Street Reform and Consumer Protection Act enacted after the world of finance did not meet social expectations. It is unclear whether the UN Sustainable Development Goals and the encyclical Laudato Si have marshalled sufficient social expectations to cause business to take these concerns very seriously. Business would be wise, however, to view these documents as embodying "soft" transnational law (Pitts *et al.*, 2009). Realizing that the impetus for this law comes not from national political discussion but from transnational civil society, the best of business leadership is moving toward forming public–privatepartnerships to meet what they take to be the legitimate social expectations of business (Elkington, 1997; Post *et al.*, 2002; Waddock, 2009).

The basis for the common theme: a common vision

This editorial argues that there is a common theme in the SDGs and the encyclical Laudato Si and that this theme is that both documents are designed to broaden the social expectations on business, to write a new social contract and reformulate the terms of the social licence to operate. How is it that the secular United Nations and the religious Vatican have a common vision for business? At root, this common vision for business flows from a common vision for society as a whole. The Preamble to the Charter of the United Nations offers a succinct statement of the UN's intention: "to reaffirm faith in fundamental human rights, in the dignity and worth of the human person ...". The religious vision of Catholic Social Teaching is summarized in a Vatican II Pastoral Constitution, *Gaudium et Spes*:

> In the economic and social realms ... the dignity and complete vocation of the human person and the welfare of society as a whole are to be respected and promoted. For man is the source, the center, and the purpose of all social life (Paul VI, 1965b, para 69).

For business, flowing from this common vision is a common understanding of the purpose of business. Catholic social thought has always taught that the single-minded focus on making money in business can never be acceptable. The purpose of business is to create sustainable value for stakeholders and that value is not exclusively monetary value (Smurthwaite, 2008; Williams, 2012). The 1991 encyclical *Centesimus Annus* expresses this broadened purpose well.

> In fact, the purpose of a business firm is not simply to make a profit, but is to be found in its very existence as a *community of persons* who in various ways are

endeavoring to satisfy their basic needs, and who form a particular group at the service of the whole society (John Paul II, 1991, para 35).

Similarly the UNGC assumes that the purpose of business is to create sustainable value for stakeholders (Freeman, 1984; Williams, 2008, 2014c; UN Global Compact, 2016). The unit of the UNGC responsible for advancing business education, the Principles for Responsible Management Education (PRME), states the purpose well: "We will develop the capabilities of students to be future generators of sustainable value for business and society at large and to work for an inclusive and sustainable global economy".[1]

Granted that the UN and religious social thought as evidenced in Laudato Si have a broadened understanding of the purpose of business (to create sustainable value for stakeholders), it goes without saying that business must respect the rights of all the key stakeholders. However, the community's understanding of the relevant rights at issue changes with the challenges of the time. The SDGs and Laudato Si are attempts to persuade the wider community that indeed the times demand more of business, that social expectations should be broadened and the social licence to operate should be more demanding.

Work as a calling

Those working to expand the social expectations on business, whether through the SDGs or Laudato Si, see their efforts as making the world a better place. These opinion leaders or average citizens understand their work as a "calling" or a "vocation" (McGee and Delbecq, 2003; Pontifical Council for Justice and Peace, 2012). (The Latin *vocare* means to call.) The meaning that people find in their work is crucial for satisfaction and the energy and motivation entailed. Perhaps a story will illustrate this point. A man was visiting a work site and he stopped and asked a worker what he was doing. "I am laying bricks", the man answered. "This is what I do all day long." He saw a second worker and asked the same question. "I am building a wall", was the reply. "I have all the tools and measurements to build a wall that will last for years." The same question was asked a third worker. "I am building a concert hall" was the reply. "In this great hall, music will play that will enable the human spirit to soar and the soul to touch the heights."

Each of these three workers had a differing orientation toward work: work as a job; work as a career; and work as a calling (Wrzesniewski, 2003; Glavas, 2014). When work is thought of as a job it is done largely for extrinsic motivation. The salary enables me to do what I really enjoy, hiking or camping, for example. Work as a career is when a student studies, masters the skills to be good in the field, and finds life personally satisfying, possessing self-esteem based on

---

1 "About Us: Six Principles".Retrieved from: http://www.unprme.org/about-prme/the-six-principles.php

successful achievements in her work. Work as a calling is present when the person has an over-arching world view and believes she is making the world a better place. The over-arching world view of Catholic Social Teaching is a call to advance the Kingdom of God and that task includes the social and political realms (Porth *et al.*, 2003). The Vatican II decree on the *Apostolate of the Laity* (*Apostolicam actuositatem*) succinctly states the view (Paul VI, 1965a, para 5):

> Christ's redemptive work, while of itself directed toward the salvation of men, involves also the renewal of the whole temporal order. Hence the mission of the Church is not only to bring to men the message and grace of Christ, but also to penetrate and perfect the temporal sphere with the spirit of the gospel. In fulfilling this mission of the Church, the laity, therefore, exercise their apostolate both in the Church and in the world, in both the spiritual and the temporal orders. These realms, although distinct, are so connected in the one plan of God that He Himself intends in Christ to appropriate the whole universe into a new creation, initially here on earth, fully on the last day. In both orders, the layman, being a believer and a citizen, should be constantly led by the same Christian conscience.

The Gospel text which underlies the notion of calling or vocation for Christians is Luke 12:48: "From everyone who has been given much, much will be demanded; and from the one who has been entrusted with much, much will be asked."

For the United Nations the over-arching world view is not a religious vision but a vision rooted in its mission to advance human rights and the dignity of the person (Arnold, 2010; Bernaz, 2012; Wettstein, 2012). These rights are stated clearly in the International Bill of Human Rights and this document is a composite of the Universal Declaration of Human Rights, the International Covenant on Civil and Political Rights, the International Covenant on Economic, Social and Cultural Rights and the International Labor Conventions. While there are some differences in the understanding of human rights on the part of the UN and the Vatican (Auza, 2016), there is consensus on the major issues in the SDGs and LS.

The parts of the whole

One way to understand the massive energy displayed by those advancing the SDGs and the vision of Laudato Si is that these people understand their efforts as a calling. The following articles exhibit various dimensions of this calling as well as the prospects for successful completion of the task.

Archbishop Auza opens the discussion by providing an overview of what Pope Francis was trying to accomplish in Laudato Si. The central theme of the encyclical is a call for dialogue on the crucial issues of our time: the plight of the poor and the ecological crisis. Based on a religious perspective, the unique contribution of Laudato Si is that it is not only an appeal to our minds but also to our hearts. In hopes that it will lead to action, Francis is writing to engage our affective dimension as well as our intellectual capacity.

Mark Moody-Stuart provides a brief overview of the founding and purpose of the United Nations Global Compact, focusing on the crucial role of the over 80 Local Networks of the UNGC. It is these Local Networks that do the primary work in forming a consensus and carrying out the action plans for the projects to make a better world. For the UN the over-arching world view is not a religious vision but the focus on human rights is largely congruent with the religious vision when it comes to action.

Jeffrey Ball offers a candid and sobering array of facts about the public's view of climate change and the influence of the encyclical. Although Laudato Si has deepened the public's knowledge about the ecological issues, there is still a long way to go before we have a consensus on how to change the global economy.

As stated earlier, many companies are motivated to advance the SDGs and ecological balance by the new social expectations for business, the business case. There are some companies, however, that have always worked toward this vision even before it was part of the social contract (Kanter, 2011). This vision is part of their mission statement, almost the DNA of the firm. The discussion of 3M by Jean Sweeney, an officer of the company, focuses on what many believe to be a firm that has always embodied much of the spirit of Laudato Si as well as a proactive stance on the SDGs. Realizing this vision is a work in progress, the essay offers many learnings for companies beginning the journey.

The article by Cavanagh is an exposition of the substance of the matter. What does the encyclical actually say and how does its vision compare with the SDGs? Cavanagh offers an excellent analysis of the document, an insightful comparison with the SDGs, as well as a discussion of the criticisms of and accolades for Laudato Si found in the press.

Martijn Cremers, a professor of finance, after examining the purpose, priority and practice of business, asks what all of this means for corporate social responsibility. He argues that "the most practical consequence for corporate social responsibility is to create a corporate environment that practices subsidiarity toward integral human development and social inclusion".

Kennedy and Calleja see Pope Francis as a shapeholder: one who has significant ability to shape the risks and opportunities of governments, international organizations and businesses. The article provides some ideas to advance global citizenship toward the poor for businesses operating in global markets.

Daniel Malan, a scholar of Integrative Social Contracts Theory, demonstrates how the theory helps to bring the universal goals of human rights to a local context in a meaningful fashion. He analyses the UNGC reports of South African companies and offers some important suggestions for improvement. For Malan, the normative component is crucial and this is to be found in the SDGs and universal values of the UNGC principles.

Walsh and Solarino, after examining the data, ask whether we can really hope that business, through the influence of the UNGC and Laudato Si, will eventually make the world a better place. The authors are cautiously optimistic and propose some actions to hasten the move toward a more just global community.

On a concluding note, the hope here is that reflecting on these articles the reader will discover a unique opportunity to grow in his or her vocation and take some action to make the world a better place.

I am most grateful to those scholars who served as reviewers for the articles in this issue, including Professors Georges Enderle, Patrick Murphy, Lisa Newton, Jerry Cavanagh, and Marilise Smurthwaite.

Finally, I want to express my gratitude to the benefactors who help to support the work of the Center for Ethics and Religious Values in Business at the University of Notre Dame, and, in particular, Michael Stephen and Bill and Beverlee Lehr. Also a thank-you is in order to Deb Coch, administrative assistant at the center, and Eric Salter, student assistant, whose work enabled this project to move from an idea to a finished product.

References

Abrams, F.W. (1951). Management responsibilities in a complex world. *Harvard Business Review*, 29(3), 29-34.

Arnold, D. (2010). Transnational corporations and the duty to respect human rights. *Business Ethics Quarterly*, 20(3), 371-399.

Auza, B. (2016). *Note of the Holy See on the First Anniversary of the Adoption of the Sustanable Development Goals.* Retrieved from: http://www.un.org/ga/search/view_doc.asp?symbol=A%2F71%2F430&Submit=search+Lang=E

Bernez, N. (2012). Enhancing corporate accountability for human rights violations: Is extraterritoriality the magic potion? *Journal of Business Ethics*, 117(3), 493-511.

Burke, R.J., Martin G., & Cooper, C.L. (2011).*Corporate Reputation: Managing Opportunities and Threats.* London: Ashgate.

Carroll, A.B. (1999). Corporate social responsibility: Evolution of a definitional construct. *Business and Society*, 38(3), 268-295.

Cragg, W. (2012). Ethics, enlightened self-interest and the corporate responsibility to respect human rights: a critical look at the justificatory foundations of the UN Framework. *Business Ethics Quarterly*, 22(1), 9-36.

Davis, K. (1960). Can business afford to ignore social responsibilities? *California Management Review*, 2(3), 70-76.

Donaldson, T. (1982). *Corporations and Morality.* Englewood Cliffs, NJ: Prentice-Hall.

Donaldson, T. (1989). *The Ethics of International Business.* Oxford: Oxford University Press.

Donaldson, T., & Dunfee, T.W. (1999). *Ties That Bind: A Social Contracts Approach to Business Ethics.* Cambridge, MA: Harvard University Business School Press.

Elkington, J. (1992). *Cannibals with Forks: The Triple-Bottom Line of 21st Century Business.* New York: Wiley & Sons.

Frederick, W.C. (2006). *Corporation Be Good: The Story of Corporate Social Responsibility.* Indianapolis, IN: Dog Ear Publishing.

Freeman, R.E. (1984). *Strategic Management: A Stakeholder Approach.* Boston, MA: Pitman.

Fukuyama, F. (1995). *The Social Virtues and the Creation of Prosperity.* New York: Free Press.

Gates, B. (2008). A new approach to capitalism. In M. Kinsley (Ed.), *Creative Capitalism: A Conversation with Bill Gates, Warren Buffett and Other Economic Leaders*(pp. 7-39). New York: Simon and Schuster.

Glavas, A. (2014). Employee engagement through social and environment responsibility. In O. Williams (Ed.), *Sustainable Development: The UN Millennium Development Goals, the UN Global Compact and the Common Good* (pp. 311-323). Notre Dame, IN: University of Notre Dame Press.

GlobeScan (1999). *The Millennium Poll on Corporate Social Responsibility: Executive Briefing.* Retrieved from:http://www.globescan.com/news_archives/MPExecBrief.pdf

Gunningham, N., Kagen, R.A., & Thornton, D. (2004). Social license and environmental protection: Why businesses go beyond compliance. *Law and Social Inquiry,* 29(2), 307-341.

Haufler, V. (2001). *A Public Role for the Private Sector: Industry Self-regulation in a Global Economy.* Washington, DC: Carnegie Endowment for International Peace.

John Paul II (1991). *Encyclical letter "CentesimusAnnus".* Vatican City: Vatican Press. Retrieved from: http://w2.vatican.va/content/john-paul-ii/en/encyclicals/documents/hf_jp-ii_enc_01051991_centesimus-annus.html

Kanter, R.M. (2011). How great companies think differently. *Harvard Business Review,* 89(11), 58-70.

Mackey, J., & Sisodia, R. (2013). *Conscious Capitalism.* Cambridge, MA: Harvard Business Review Press.

Matten, D., & Moon, J. (2008). "Implicit and explicit" CSR: A conceptual framework for a comparative understanding of corporate social responsibility. *Academy of Management Review,* 33(2), 404-424.

Mayer, R.C., Davis, J.H., & Schoorman, F.D. (1995). An interactive model of organizational trust. *Academy of Management Review,* 20(3), 709-734.

McGee, J., & Delbecq, A. (2003). Vocation as a critical factor in a spirituality for executive leadership in business. In O. Williams (Ed.), *Business, Religion, and Spirituality* (pp. 94-110).Notre Dame, IN: University of Notre Dame Press.

Nelsen, J.L. (2006). Social license to operate. *International Journal of Mining, Reclamation and Environment,* 20(3), 161-162.

Paine, L.S. (2003). *Value Shift: Why Companies Must Merge Social and Financial Imperatives to Achieve Superior Performance.* New York: McGraw-Hill.

Palazzo, G., & Scherer, A. (2006). Corporate legitimacy as deliberation: A communicative framework. *Journal of Business Ethics,* 66(1), 71-88.

Paul VI (1965a, November 18). *Decree on the Apostolate of the Laity: Apostolicam Actuositatem.* Retrieved from: http://www.vatican.va/archive/hist_councils/ii_vatican_council/documents/vat-ii_decree_19651118_apostolicam-actuositatem_en.html

Paul VI (1965b, December 7). *The Pastoral Constitution on the Church in the Modern World: Gaudium et Spes.* Retrieved from: http://www.vatican.va/archive/hist_councils/ii_vatican_council/documents/vat-ii_cons_19651207_gaudium-et-spes_en.html

Pitts, C., Kerr, M., & Janda, R. (2009). *Corporate Social Responsibility: A Legal Analysis.* Canada: LexisNexis.

Pontifical Council for Justice and Peace (2012).*Vocation of the Business Leader: A Reflection.* Retrieved from: http://www.stthomas.edu/media/catholicstudies/center/ryan/publications/publicationpdfs/vocationofthebusinessleaderpdf/PontificalCouncil_4.pdf

Porter, M.,& Kramer, M. (2011). Creating shared value. *Harvard Business Review,* 89, 62-77.

Porth, S.J., Steingard, D., & McCall, J. (2003). Spirituality and business: The latest management fad or a new breakthrough? In O. Williams (Ed.), *Business, Religion, and Spirituality* (pp. 255-260). Notre Dame, IN: University of Notre Dame Press.

Post, J.E., Preston, L.E., & Sachs, S. (2002). *Redefining the Corporation.* Stanford, CA: Stanford University Press.

Prno, J., & Slocombe, D.S. (2012). Exploring the origins of "social license to operate" in the mining sector: Perspectives from governance and sustainability theories. *Resource Policy,* 37, 346-357.

Ruggie, J. (2013). *Just Business.* Boston, MA: Norton Publishers.

Smurthwaite, M. (2008). The purpose of the corporation. In O. Williams (Ed.), *Peace Through Commerce* (pp. 13-54). Notre Dame, IN: University of Notre Dame Press.

UN (2008, April 7). *Protect, Respect and Remedy: A Framework for Business and Human Rights.* UN Doc. A/HRC/8/5 (2008). Geneva: United Nations.

UN (2011, March 21). *Guiding Principles on Business and Human Rights: Implementing the United Nations "Protect, Respect, Remedy" Framework,* UN Doc. A/HRC/17/31. Geneva: United Nations.

UN Global Compact (2016). *Homepage.* Retrieved from: http://www.unglobalcompact.org

Velasquez, M.G. (2015). *Business Ethics: Concepts and Cases.* Upper Saddle River, NJ: Pearson Prentice Hall.

Vogel, D. (2005). *The Market for Virtue: The Potential and Limits of Corporate Social Responsibility.* Washington, DC: Brookings Institution Press.

Waddock, S. (2009). *Leading Corporate Citizens: Vision, Values, Value-Added* (3rd ed.). New York: McGraw-Hill.

Wettstein, F. (2012). CSR and the debate on business and human rights: Bridging the great divide. *Business Ethics Quarterly,* 22(4), 739-770.

Williams, O. (2004). The UN Global Compact: The challenge and the promise. *Business Ethics Quarterly,* 14(4), 755-774.

Williams, O. (2008). Responsible corporate citizenship and the ideals of the United Nations Global Compact. In O. Williams (Ed.), *Peace through Commerce* (pp. 431-452). Notre Dame, IN: University of Notre Dame Press.

Williams, O. (2012). Is it possible to have a business based on solidarity and mutual trust? *Journal of Catholic Social Thought,* 9(1), 59-69.

Williams, O. (2014a). The United Nations Global Compact: What did it promise? *Journal of Business Ethics,* 25(122), 241-251.

Williams, O. (2014b). *Corporate Social Responsibility: The Role of Business in Sustainable Development.* New York: Routledge.

Williams, O. (2014c). CSR: Will it change the world? *Journal of Corporate Citizenship,* 18(53), 9-26.

Wrzesniewski, A. (2003). Finding positive meaning in work. In K.S. Cameron, J.E. Dutton & R.E. Quinn (Eds.), *Positive Organizational Scholarship: Foundations of a New Discipline* (pp. 296-308). San Francisco: Berrett-Koehler.

Zadek, S. (2004). The path to corporate responsibility. *Harvard Business Review,* 82(12), 2-10.

DOI: [10.9774/GLEAF.4700.2016.de.00004]

An Overview from the Point of View of Pope Francis

Archbishop Bernardito Auza

United Nations, USA

Representing Pope Francis to the United Nations has afforded me the privilege to participate in the 2015 international conferences that were meant to define the trajectory of development for at least the next 15 years. From Addis Ababa in July, to New York in September, to Paris in December, heads of state or government committed themselves to sustainable development while caring for the environment. Many appealed to the moral authority of Pope Francis on questions like extreme poverty and the environment, economic systems and social inequalities, disarmament and underdevelopment. These huge issues may look vastly different from one another, but as Pope Francis insists in the Encyclical Laudato Si, they are all interconnected and are merely different faces of an integral "human ecology". The comprehensive solutions we seek to face these problems should consider not only the present generation, but also future generations and everything in creation. If we are to achieve positive global outcomes, we have to recognize this interdependence. To arrive at comprehensive solutions, Pope Francis is calling everyone to an honest dialogue. The term "dialogue" is ubiquitous in the Encyclical, as the Holy Father aimed to provide impetus to discussions at every level, with the then more immediate purpose of building momentum towards reaching a global climate deal in Paris—which succeeded—and the long-term vision of helping us interiorize, so to speak, love and care for our common home. Pope Francis is calling for transformative action that goes beyond business as usual, an interdisciplinary approach that will bring together science and religion, philosophy and culture, the humanities and technology, economics and politics, individuals and groups. The Pope repeated this call in Nairobi on the eve of the Paris Conference, putting greater pressure on the international community by affirming that it would be tragic if in Paris special interests were to win over the common good. Although there is environmental and social degradation in far too many places, Pope Francis is rallying us to stay hopeful. (LS, 205).

- Dialogue
- Integral ecology
- Transformative action
- The poor

Archbishop Bernardito Auza is Papal Nuncio and Permanent Observer of the Holy See to the United Nations. Born in the Philippines, he was ordained a priest in 1985. The Archbishop joined the diplomatic service of the Holy See in 1990, serving in different capacities successively in Madagascar and Mauritius, Bulgaria, Albania, the Secretariat of State in the Vatican (1998–2006) and the Permanent Observer Mission of the Holy See to the United Nations in New York (2006–2008). In May 2008 Archbishop Auza was named Papal Nuncio to Haiti. He was consecrated an Archbishop in 2008 at Saint Peter's Basilica in the Vatican. In July 2014 Pope Francis appointed him Permanent Observer of the Holy See to the United Nations in New York and Permanent Observer of the Holy See to the Organization of American States in Washington, DC.

nuntius@holyseemission.org

A culture of dialogue and encounter

Pope Francis has travelled and addressed international questions much more than most would have expected at the beginning of his Pontificate. As of July 2016, he had already visited 21 countries in all the continents except Oceania: from war-torn Central African Republic to the United States, from Cuba to the Philippines, from South Korea to Mexico. He has already addressed the Council of Europe, a Joint Session of US Congress and the United Nations General Assembly.

People pause to listen to his words and many act on them because, as Catholics and non-Catholics often admit, they see him as a credible leader, a moral authority, a persuasive teacher, an authentic "Pontifex" or bridge-builder.

I see one golden thread tying all the words and actions of Pope Francis together, a unifying inspiration that has overarching implications not only on the pastoral and spiritual activities of the Church, but also on primary socioeconomic and political concerns of our time.

That golden thread would be the theme and practice of encounter, of dialogue, of building bridges rather than walls, of the globalization of solidarity over a globalization of indifference. While still Archbishop of Buenos Aires, the future Pope said that one of the most fundamental characteristics of a fundamentalist is hatred of dialogue. The fundamentalist prefers monologues to dialogue, speaking to listening, and imposing his views on others in a unidirectional way. A fundamentalist does not know what dialogue is.

Pope Francis's address to the United Nations General Assembly on 25 September 2015 could not have been other than a speech to strengthen bridges and tear down walls. After enumerating some of the major achievements of the United Nations as it was celebrating its 70th year of foundation, the Pope said that, while many problems have remained unresolved, every achievement has been "a path towards attaining the ideal of human fraternity and a means for its greater realization".

The United Nations is a symbol, place and vehicle for the cooperation of all the countries and nations of the world. It is not perfect; it needs serious reforms. A former high-ranking UN authority recently said in an ironic manner, "I care deeply for the principles the United Nations is designed to uphold. And that's why I have decided to leave". Thanks to "colossal mismanagement", he added, "the United Nations is failing" (Banbury, 2016).

But as many would say, if the United Nations or a similar forum did not exist, it would have to be invented. Pope Francis himself said that while the structure and activities of the United Nations can be improved, "it remains necessary, if mankind [is] to survive the unchecked use of its own possibilities". It's a rather scary thought that we must have a body like to UN to keep our own Leviathans at bay!

Pope Francis relates the culture of encounter to solidarity. That is why, when he discusses issues with political implications, he constantly affirms a diplomacy of encounter, a diplomacy of dialogue capable of realizing unity and fighting exclusion, a diplomacy of *caminar juntos* as a way of life. A culture of encounter is not possible with walls and isolationism, but only with bridges and open doors.

But many ask: Why does the Pope care so much about issues with strong political and socioeconomic policy implications?

The answer is simple: Because Jesus cares! And if Jesus cares, the Church cannot but care. There is nothing genuinely human that is alien to the Church. As the celebrated opening passage of the Second Vatican Council's *Gaudium et Spes* affirms:

> The joys and the hopes, the griefs and the anxieties of the men of this age, especially those who are poor or in any way afflicted, these are the joys and hopes, the griefs and anxieties of the followers of Christ. Indeed, nothing genuinely human fails to raise an echo in their hearts (Paul VI, 1965).

Laudato Si: an invitation to dialogue

The term "dialogue" is ubiquitous in the Encyclical Laudato Si. It is present in every chapter. In particular, Chapter V suggests dialogue on "lines of approach and action" on the environment in the international community, in national and local policies, in decision-making, in politics and economy, and of religions with science. He calls these "lines of approach and action" as "paths of dialogue" (LS, 163) toward finding an "urgent response and a radical change in humanity's behavior" to avert an "ecological crisis" (LS, 4).

The Pope's view of Laudato Si as an instrument of dialogue is obvious from the start of the Encyclical. As we know, an encyclical literally means a "circular letter". Traditionally, a Papal Encyclical is addressed to the bishops, priests, religious men and women, and to all the faithful. Pope Francis explicitly affirms, however, "In this Encyclical, I would like to enter into dialogue with all the people about our common home" (LS, 3).

Pope Francis wants to bring into conversation individuals and entire societies, state institutions and civic organizations, each one bringing its specific contribution. In an increasingly globalized and complex world, different perspectives are ever more intertwined and complementary—the riches of faith and of spiritual tradition, the seriousness of scientific research, the concrete efforts at various levels of both government and civil society—and all must be brought together to foster equitable and sustainable development.

The Pope calls for transformative action that goes beyond business as usual and that will bring together science and religion, the humanities and technology, philosophy and culture, economics and politics, persons and groups, states and civil society, prayers and Instagram, mercy and Twitter, dialogue across the dining table and dialogue through Facebook.

This conference is a response to that call to interdisciplinary dialogue and collaboration. Together with Pope Francis, the University of Notre Dame and the

UN Global Compact believe that we need a conversation that includes everyone, so that we can collaboratively meet the huge development and environmental challenges of today.

Dialogue that leads to empathy with the suffering nature and humanity

The Pope calls us not only to dialogue with one another but also with nature itself. He wants us to listen carefully to its groanings and to dare to turn those groanings into our own personal suffering (LS, 19).

This call to develop empathy with all of God's creation is evocative of St Francis of Assisi, who preached to the birds and tamed wolves. Because this element of communion with all of God's creation is so fundamental to his message, Pope Francis took the title of Laudato Si from the Canticle of the Creatures that Saint Francis composed in 1225 while ill at San Damiano. "Laudato Sie, mi Signore cum tucte le Tue creature". "Praise be to you, My Lord, with all your creatures!"

In praising the Lord with all his creatures, Saint Francis reminds us that the Earth, our common home, is, the Pope asserts, "like a sister with whom we share our life and a beautiful mother who opens her arms to embrace us" (LS, 1). Pope Francis invites us to look towards the "poor one of Assisi" as a source of inspiration because he is

> ... the example par excellence of care for the vulnerable and of an integral ecology lived out joyfully and authentically. [...] He shows us just how inseparable is the bond between concern for nature, justice for the poor, commitment to society, and interior peace (LS, 10).

This empathy with the natural world that is suffering because of our irresponsible actions should bring us to action, and should arouse in our hearts an empathy with the poor who are most vulnerable to climate change at least partly caused by us, empathy with those who have been adversely affected by economic activities that have damaged nature, empathy with those who have been affected by environmental degradation or who are excluded from economic and political processes.

Pope Francis launches a particular challenge to public authorities not to respond merely to financial powers and economic systems purely in pursuit of profit provoking environmental damage. The Pope wonders: "What would induce anyone, at this stage, to hold on to power only to be remembered for their inability to take action when it was urgent and necessary to do so?" (LS, 57).

I am sure that the Holy Father was pleased that the United Nations Global Compact, reacting to Laudato Si, has concurred that "isolated pursuit of profit distorts the concept of economy and threatens our common home", and has embraced "the call to create a more just and sustainable global economy".

The need for an integral ecology

The objective of the Global Compact to give a human face to the global market is one way of expressing the value of solidarity that is so central to the idea of integral ecology.

Pope Francis puts integral ecology at the centre of the Encyclical as a paradigm able to articulate the fundamental multidimensionality of our relationships: our relationships with one another, our relationship with God, and our relationship with creation as a whole.

That's why when the Pope uses the term "environment", he does not only refer to nature, but to a complex of realities and relationships. Nature cannot be regarded as something separate from ourselves or as a mere setting in which we live. We are part of nature, included in it and thus in constant interaction with it. A crisis of the environment necessarily means a crisis for humanity. "We are not faced with two separate crises, one environmental and the other social, but rather one complex crisis that is both social and environmental", he said. Thus, "Strategies for a solution demand an integrated approach to combating poverty, restoring dignity to the excluded, and at the same time protecting nature" (LS, 139).

I believe the idea of integral ecology is the axis of the Encyclical around which all the other thoughts rotate and from which they emanate. The principle of interconnectedness is picked up and continuously enriched from different perspectives, such as the intimate relationship between the poor and the fragility of the planet; the value proper to each creature and their place in the scale of creation; the importance of biodiversity; the human meaning of ecology; the anthropological and environmental consequences of the throwaway culture; the invitation to search for other ways of understanding economy and progress; the need for intergenerational solidarity; and so on.

The principle of interconnectedness is also found in the three biggest United Nations processes in 2015, namely the Addis Ababa Action Agenda on financing for development, the 2030 Agenda for Sustainable Development, and the Paris Agreement on Climate Change. There are not three separate challenges of financing development needs, agreeing on new development goals and tackling climate change, but one overarching challenge of how to orient our politics, economies, technology and businesses—indeed, all our efforts—towards an integral and authentic development in harmony with nature. As the Open Letter of the United Nations Global Compact to Pope Francis in response to Laudato Si rightly affirms, "The challenges threatening the earth's survival are far too great for any one sector or institution to address alone" (Kell *et al.*, 2015).

It is through this perspective that economics should transcend the approach of considering nature as mere resources and peoples as mere manufacturing machines to be put under the headings of assets or liabilities.

In order to promote integral ecology within the political-economic global system, we need a new approach to national and global politics that goes beyond traditional silos and the traditional primacy of economic decisions. It means that we don't simply ask *how much money* is needed for development or where it will come from, but *how do we ensure that we are promoting a development* that is integral, authentic and sustainable.

Thanks to this integrated approach to questions related to economic, social and environmental development, we can find in the Encyclical a convergence of ethics, theology, empirical science and even of rhetoric and poetic prose for an integral ecology. With an eye to the Post-2015 Development Summit and to the Paris Conference, Pope Francis called on all national and world leaders and on international organizations to add to this convergence of elements a firm, united political will to save ourselves from "business as usual" and from a "spiral of self-destruction". The international community has manifested this firm, united political will in the strong commitments contained in the 2030 Agenda for Sustainable Development and in the Paris Agreement. We need to work to ensure that they won't remain pious intentions.

The moral imperative to care for our common home

At the heart of the Encyclical we find this question: "What kind of world do we want to leave to those who come after us, to children who are now growing up?" It is a question that does not have to do with the environment in isolation. It begs the deepest questions about the meaning of our existence and the values that must lead us to an "ecological conversion", according to the expression of St John Paul II, that is, a change of direction by taking on beautiful responsibility of caring for our common home.

It is because of his firm belief in our capacity to change direction that Pope Francis concludes Laudato Si with an uplifting challenge. Although our common home is falling into serious disrepair, we can reverse the trend of environmental degradation, he insists, because while we are capable of the worst, we are also capable of the best, rising above ourselves, choosing again what is good, and making a new start (LS, 13, 58 and 205).

The conviction that we are capable of the best is not based on utilitarian calculations, nor even on what empirical science tells us about the condition that the environment is in; rather, it is anchored in a moral imperative flowing from a profound theological truth: to love and care for creation because it is God's gift for us.

Thus the Holy Father dedicates the whole second chapter of Laudato Si to the great biblical narrative of Creation. The biggest single challenge that can determine our individual and common response to a "crisis in integral ecology" is not scientific or technological, but rather is found within our minds and hearts. The Creation narrative says a lot about who we are, our relationship with God, with the world and with one another, and thus possesses an enduring power to open new horizons, to stimulate our thoughts, and to expand our minds and hearts towards an ever greater care and ever deeper love for our common home.

Inspired by the Creation narrative, both Saint Francis of Assisi and Pope Francis are leading us in singing "Laudato Si, mi Signore, con tutte le tue creature". "Praise be to you, Lord, with all your creatures".

References

Banbury, A. (2016, March 18). I love the U.N., but it is failing. *The New York Times*. Retrieved from: http://www.nytimes.com/2016/03/20/opinion/sunday/i-love-the-un-but-it-is-failing.html

Francis I (2015). *Encyclical letter "Laudato Si": On Care for Our Common Home*. Vatican City: Vatican Press. Retrieved from: http://w2.vatican.va/content/francesco/en/encyclicals/documents/papa-francesco_20150524_enciclica-laudato-si.html

Kell, G., Kingo, L., & Reynolds, F. (2015, August 7). *Open Letter to His Holiness Pope Francis from the United Nations Global Compact Responding to Laudato Si*. Retrieved from: https://www.unglobalcompact.org/docs/issues_doc/Environment/Laudato_Si_Open_Letter_UN_Global_Compact.pdf

Paul VI (1965b, December 7). *The Pastoral Constitution on the Church in the Modern World: Gaudium et Spes*. Retrieved from: http://www.vatican.va/archive/hist_councils/ii_vatican_council/documents/vat-ii_cons_19651207_gaudium-et-spes_en.html

DOI: [10.9774/GLEAF.4700.2016.de.00005]

An Overview from the Point of View of the UN Global Compact

Mark Moody-Stuart

Global Compact Foundation, USA

From the Papal Encyclical to the Sustainable Development Goals the need for wide societal engagement is clear. The United Nations Global Compact (UNGC) and its Local Networks are a powerful means of achieving this. The Rana Plaza disaster shows the need for such diverse input. If the Independently Determined National Commitments made on climate in Paris in December 2015 are to be achieved, wide support from business and civil society is needed. Establishing regulatory frameworks to guide the creativity of the market in societally desirable directions requires similar support and the UNGC Local Networks are an important mechanism to achieve this. Responsible business can maintain engagement across fractious political boundaries and examples are given where this may be more effective than economic sanctions. The risks of such engagement are discussed along with an outline of what responsibility means in this context. It is suggested that businesses can be contributors to peace.

● UN Global Compact

● UNGC Local Network

● Universal values

● Sustainable Development Goals

● Laudato Si

Mark Moody-Stuart is Chairman of the Board of Directors of the Global Compact Foundation and of the Innovative Vector Control Consortium (IVCC). He was the Chairman of the Royal Dutch/Shell Group (1998– 2001), of Anglo American plc (2002– 09), and of Hermes Equity Ownership Services (2009–16). After a doctorate in geology, he worked for Shell living in Holland, Spain, Oman, Brunei, Australia, Nigeria, Turkey, Malaysia and the UK. Currently he is a director of Saudi Aramco (2007–) and was a director of Accenture (2001–15) and HSBC (2001–10). He also serves as the Chairman of the FTSE ESG Advisory Committee, Vice Chairman of the United Nations Global Compact Board, Honorary Co-Chairman of the International Tax and Investment Center (2011–) and a Member of the International Council for Integrated Reporting. He is the author of *Responsible Leadership: Lessons from the Front Line of Sustainability and Ethics*. He is married to Judy and they have four children.

markmoodystuart@msmjc.com

MORE THAN 15 YEARS AGO in 1999, the then Secretary-General of the UN, Kofi Annan, issued a challenge to businesses. He said "I propose that you, the business leaders gathered in Davos, and we, the United Nations, initiate a global compact of shared values and principles, which will give a human face to the global market" (Annan, 1999). He went on to say "Specifically, I call on you—individually through your firms, and collectively through your business associations—to embrace, support and enact a set of core values in the areas of human rights, labour standards, and environmental practices". He also committed to the business leaders that in the United Nations "we are ready to facilitate a dialogue between you and other social groups, to help find viable solutions to the genuine concerns that they have raised".

Out of this challenge grew the UN Global Compact (UNGC), with an initial nine principles based on the major UN Conventions on human rights, labour and the environment, with a tenth principle on fighting corruption added when the UN Convention against Corruption was signed in 2003. Initially some 40 global companies took up the challenge, working from the beginning with labour and civil society organizations to see how these high level principles could be incorporated into their day-to-day operations. As of 2016, with the strong support of the former UN Secretary-General Ban Ki-Moon, the Compact has grown to have some 8,500 business signatories with a further 4,000 supporting civil society and labour organizations in over 100 countries.

The unique features of the UNGC

There are three unique features of the UN Global Compact which separate it from many other excellent organizations such as the World Economic Forum or the World Business Council for Sustainable Development. First, it is grounded on the ten principles which reflect universal values embodied in numerous UN Conventions. These values are agreed to by all member states, even if the behaviour of governments often falls far short of these ideals. Second, UNGC is inclusive, embracing not only businesses of all sizes in most countries, but in involving from the outset civil society and labour organizations in its governance structure. Third, all the businesses commit to reporting publicly and transparently on the progress and development in embedding the principles into their day-to-day operations. I believe that there is no other organization which combines these three critical features—a basis of fundamental values, inclusive of business of all sizes and of all sectors of society, which, moreover, commits to transparency and open public reporting.

Landmark events in 2015 promoting popular engagement

The year 2015 was remarkable for a number of landmark events. The first was the publication in May of the Papal Encyclical "Laudato Si on Advancing Care for Our Common Home". This was followed in September by the unanimous adoption by the Member States of the United Nations of the Sustainable Development Goals. Then in Paris in December there was the agreement to combat climate change with an ambition of holding global temperature rise to less than 2 degrees Celsius above pre-industrial levels.

There is a common theme linking all of these events as well as the UN Global Compact, namely the need for wide engagement and collective action by all sections of society. In his Encyclical Pope Francis notes that "Humanity still has the ability to work together in building our common home" (Laudato Si, 13) and that "we need a conversation which includes everyone" (LS, 14). He goes on to say that "many efforts to seek concrete solutions have proved ineffective, not only because of powerful opposition but also because of a more general lack of interest" (LS, 14). The process of arriving at the Sustainable Development Goals was one of the most inclusive ever undertaken by the UN, with thousands of opportunities for members of the public to participate. The UN Global Compact was itself a focal point for input from business and others to the process. The bulk of the commitments made on climate in Paris are in the form of Intended Nationally Determined Contributions (INDCs) whereby each country commits to a series of actions to combat climate change.

In the Open Letter from the UNGC in response to the Encyclical, Lise Kingo and Georg Kell of the UNGC and Fiona Reynolds of the UN Principles for Responsible Investment suggested that the UNGC and its networked based infrastructure could act as a bridge between the Encyclical's vision of integral ecology with practical efforts to mobilize responsible business. They affirmed that:

> People are at the heart of all business, and those who recognize the power and influence of their own humanity can do tremendous good. Today's global market is a complex array of deeply integrated chains of value. Large corporations are connected to countless smaller businesses. No enterprise can sustain itself in isolation. The fabric of global commerce consists of small and mid-sized businesses, cooperatives of many sizes, state-owned enterprise, multinationals, and informal economies. People lead them all and all are enabled by the varied contributions of people (Kell *et al.*, 2015).

The role of the UNGC Local Networks in achieving a more sustainable world

So what role can the UNGC play in practice towards a more sustainable world? The UNGC is the world's largest business-led multi-stakeholder organization committed to responsible business, with its 8,500 business signatories and some 4,000 other organizations. There is no doubt that its issue platforms, such as "Caring for Climate", the CEO Water Mandate, Human Rights and Labour Working Group, and Supply Chain Working Group, bring together smaller groups of businesses committed to improving business impact in such areas, make significant commitments and contributions. But to put this in perspective, 8,500 businesses are only about 10% of the total of truly global multinationals and a very small proportion of the significant national businesses and the millions of small and medium sized enterprises (SMEs).

This is why the growth of the UNGC Local Networks is so important. There are currently over 80 Local Networks which bring together businesses large and small, national and global, as well as civil society and labour organizations. Within the networks affiliates of major global companies can demonstrate how the highest international standards in working conditions and in transparency can contribute to business performance, while those same companies can learn from responsible national businesses committed to the UNGC how the principles can be promoted in a way congruent with the national culture. All companies, large and small, benefit from the development of local supply chains. It is only in and through the Local Networks that the very many smaller businesses can be actively engaged and examples of good practice and the business benefits can be demonstrated in companies of all sizes across a country.

A lesson from the Rana Plaza disaster

Achievement of the Sustainable Development Goals requires action in each and every country. Take the example of the garment industry in Bangladesh. The tragedy of the collapse of the Rana Plaza factory on 24 April 2013, in which 1,130 people died, was unfortunately not an isolated event. Reoccurrences will only be prevented in the future by collective action of international garment businesses working with local factory owners to ensure safe buildings. Labour unions have clearly played an important part in driving this process forward (the major union groups involved are represented on the board of the UNGC). The government too must play its part through proper and impartial enforcement of standards. Some considerable time before the Rana Plaza event I had a meeting with the Bangladesh UNGC Local Network. Their two priority areas of work were the conditions for Bangladeshi migrant workers in the Gulf States (a concern which was incidentally also a priority for the Emirates Local Network) and also the mutual benefits of employing physically disabled workers. I suspect that had more local affiliates of major global players in the garment industry, or indeed local labour unions, been active in the Local Network, the question of working conditions and factory building safety might have been higher on the agenda and perhaps even tragedy avoided. The advantage of Local Networks comes from the diversity of involvement, of companies large and small, national and international and of civil society and labour organizations. That is the goal.

Support needed for market-guiding frameworks

There is another important role for Local Networks and indeed for the leadership of businesses globally. If governments are to meet their INDCs present as part of the Paris Climate Agreement, or indeed if they are to establish the rational frameworks necessary to guide the creativity of the market in socially desirable directions, support from different constituents is essential.

I am a great believer in the power of markets to deliver choice to members of society and also through competition to be a mechanism for allocating resources and stimulating creativity. But there are some things that the market will not deliver on its own. These are things which deliver no immediate benefits to the individual consumer or company concerned, but which benefit society as a whole. Such things need regulatory frameworks, imposed by governments, which can guide the creativity of the market and competition in societally desirable directions. Examples are the auto catalysts which clean up vehicle exhausts and the frameworks necessary to put a price on carbon.

An exhaust catalyst on the back of a vehicle adds no immediate benefit to the vehicle owner, although some to the driver behind, while it adds a couple of hundred dollars to the price of the vehicle. Yet the benefit to society at large is considerable. On a recent visit to Tehran where there are basically no catalysts, I could smell the unburnt gasoline in the traffic jams which plague all major cities. The fitting of catalysts would never have been achieved without regulation, although it is now universal in developed markets. Similarly, if there is to be a rational market mechanism to encourage the development of energy sources which emit less carbon dioxide to the atmosphere, there needs to be a carbon price to drive the market. Such a price, whether national or global, can only be achieved by government regulation mandating a carbon tax or the framework for a cap and trade system. To achieve greater societal benefits, markets need regulatory frameworks that channel the creativity of the market in a desirable direction without tying the hands of business by specifying the preferred technology or method but only the standard that must be achieved.

In establishing such market-guiding frameworks, governments are subject to pressures from two directions. The first is from consumers, who are also voters, who want convenience at the lowest cost. The framework has to be one acceptable to voters. On the other hand, governments are also normally cognizant of the views of business, who may object on the grounds of international competitiveness or may threaten that it will damage the economy and cost jobs.

The role of UNGC Local Networks in supporting development of frameworks

In this process, the UNGC and its Local Networks can play an important role, by bringing together responsible businesses from different sectors with civil society and labour organizations. The UNGC and its Local Networks can encourage governments and help build the courage necessary to establish such rational frameworks. Because of the diversity of parties involved, the almost inevitable special pleading by particular industry sectors particularly impacted by regulation is avoided. Likewise, the possible undue emphasis placed by some civil society organizations focused narrowly on a single objective can be overcome. This support for government action in building rational frameworks can be constructed collectively at either local level through Local Networks, taking into account the particular national conditions, or globally through the UNGC's issue platforms. Thus the UNGC and its "Caring for Climate" platform was an important contributor to the Paris climate process. Equally businesses and Local Networks nationally have a role to play in helping governments achieve the INDCs committed to in Paris. Less successful in the end, but of critical importance in bringing the issue to the table, was the UNGC's support for carbon pricing in some form, whether by a carbon tax, or a framework for a cap and trade system. An important role of business leaders is to take off their corporate hat and put on their societal hat when such frameworks are being developed. Once the framework is established, businesses can exercise creativity and ingenuity in developing products and processes which win in the market within that framework.

Maintaining commercial relationships in contrast to economic sanctions

There is another role that responsible businesses which subscribe to the ten principles of the UNGC can play; that is maintaining civilized commercial relationships across fractious political boundaries. I attended a recent launch of the UNGC's Business for Peace platform in Khartoum in Sudan. There were some excellent examples of responsible Sudanese businesses working to build businesses and community relations in post-conflict areas. For example, a Sudanese business which required peanuts as input into food mixtures for its high-quality milk herd in Khartoum was sourcing these from Darfur and building enterprises there in areas of previous conflict. I was very encouraged to see business representative of the newly separated South Sudan attending the meeting and working with their counterparts to maintain trade and business relationships across a very difficult political boundary. This is essential, because without such trade links neither country will truly thrive. The same is true of Ukraine. The relationships between Ukraine and Russia over Crimea and the eastern regions of Ukraine are understandably fractious and at times unfortunately lethal. Yet the interconnections in water, gas, electricity and fuel are critical. The dependency on power generation from another area to be supplied to another area and the need for fuel for those power stations from a third area, mean that rational commercial arrangements are essential to any sustainable solution to conflict.

These arrangements can be developed by responsible business people speaking the same language of business and of human understanding across boundaries.

Unfortunately, the common Western response of applying economic sanctions to those countries with governments of which we do not approve militates against rational and responsible business development. Economic sanctions are an understandable response to the popular frustration with inactivity, but they can have unintended consequences. Consider the case of Iran which has been subject to economic sanctions of one sort or another since the Iranian revolution more than 35 years ago. This has allowed a generally unattractive regime to find an outside enemy to blame for all its failings. As economic activity shrank, the private sector, which included many responsible Iranian companies, also shrank and was reduced in influence. The government and its Basij militia, which numbers around a million activists, have gained influence and the government has used the limited economic activity remaining as a lever in its hands. Businesses and those who favour a more liberal and open approach have been pushed aside. The result has thus been entirely counterproductive. Many would argue that only recently through the tightened sanctions has it been possible to force negotiations on the nuclear issue. While this is probably true, it has come at the cost of 30 years of damage to an economy and well-developed society. The recent response of the Iranian electorate suggests that had there been continued constructive engagement, including economic engagement, the change might have come earlier.

The history of Myanmar also suggests that engagement is better than isolation. While the Western nations applied sanctions, the members of the ASEAN nations continued to engage while pointing out the disadvantages of the Myanmar Government's approach. Indications are that engagement, perhaps linked with concern over growing Chinese influence, did more than sanctions to bring about positive change. Part of the opening of Myanmar has been the establishment of an active UNGC Local Network, with the blessing of the government, encouraging businesses to operate in line with the ten principles of the UNGC.

I believe that the long-term engagement of the oil company Total in Myanmar resulted in something of a change of attitude to such engagement. Although certainly initially heavily criticized because of human rights abuses by government connected forces along the gas export pipeline, Total stayed the course. When Cyclone Nargis struck in 2008, many civil society organizations found that Total and its operations were one of the few functioning parts of the economy and were able to build on that to bring much needed aid to devastated areas. Previously, in contrast, similar controversial engagement by the Canadian company Talisman in Sudan had resulted in pressure for the company to withdraw. Talisman sold its Sudanese interests to a consortium of Chinese, Malaysian and Indian companies, who although able and responsible operators, were less inclined to engage with critics. In the light of this, people began to see the advantages of engagement by responsible companies prepared to be open about their operations and the impacts.

I think that we should all be grateful that the outcome of the Nixon and Kissinger visit to China, a country in which many thousands had died through the actions of the government, was opening up of trade relations rather than isolation through sanctions. Perhaps the difference was due to the size of the country. Whatever the reason, this opening up embraced by China has benefitted hundreds of millions of people.

The risks of such engagement—dining with the devil

The engagement of businesses across fractious political boundaries is not without its risks. The leader of any major business operating in a country is likely to have occasion to meet the head of state and have discussions. The individual head of state may well be someone who has at least in the past if not currently been accused of responsibility for human rights abuses or corruption. This is what I call "dining with the devil". If a company or its leadership is to have any positive influence, such engagement is necessary. Maintaining and expressing one's own values and those of the company is vital and yet, if one is to have any positive influence, it is essential to establish a personal connection of some sort. This can be difficult and is likely to be controversial. Three hundred and fifty years ago George Fox advised the fledgling Quakers to …

> Be patterns, be examples in all countries, places, islands, nations, wherever you come, that your carriage and life may preach among all sorts of people, and to them; then you will come to walk cheerfully over the world, answering that of God in every one (Quaker Faith and Practice. fifth Edition Chapter 19.32).

Those of secular inclination might prefer to replace "preach" with "be an example to" and perhaps "that of God" with "humanity", but it remains excellent advice. More recently Martin Luther King said "You have very little moral persuasive power with people who can feel your underlying contempt". However, this influence can work both ways; strong and openly expressed values are an important part of the defence.

What defines a responsible company?

If there are benefits of responsible businesses engaging across fractious political borders and operating in countries whose governments are, to say the least, highly controversial, what are the yardsticks by which we could judge a "responsible company"? Clearly no human organization is perfect, but a business is more likely to be responsible if it subscribes to principles such as those of the UNGC and works to embed them throughout its day-to-day operations wherever in the world. An essential further step is to be open and public in reporting in its progress in that area, as is required by the UNGC's Communications on Progress. In relation to its operations in the particular country concerned a responsible business needs to be very open to discussion and engagement with civil society and human rights organizations. The potential to be held to account by shareholders and by consumers is also an important factor. So such a company is more likely to be a public company than a state-owned operation or a privately owned company, although there are both highly responsible state-owned and privately owned companies.

Conclusions

In conclusion, as Pope Francis stated in Laudato Si, "we need a conversation which includes everyone" (LS, 14). There need to be clearly expressed guiding principles. The UNGC Local Networks acting within the framework of the ten principles based on the major conventions of the UN are an important means of achieving this collaborative approach on issues of priority in each country. Support from businesses, in coalition with civil society and labour organizations, is important in giving governments the courage to develop the frameworks necessary to channel market forces in societally useful directions.

Taking this further, responsible businesses can contribute to building peaceful relationships across fractious political boundaries. For example, International Alert has done much good work in building better relationships across borders between countries in the South Caucasus, involving collective export and marketing of products from different countries. I was struck by a slogan used in that area "When we say Peace, we mean Business".

There are many encouraging examples of this sort from Local Networks in the UNGC platform "Business for Peace". At the first annual Business for Peace meeting in Istanbul in 2014 which brought together examples from many different countries, the Korean Global Compact Network demonstrated the work of the Gaesong Industrial Complex developed by South Korean companies in an enclave of North Korea. Here some 55,000 North Korean workers work in excellent conditions in modern manufacturing facilities run by over 200 South Korean companies, producing mainly textiles and footwear. This project is not without controversy as it can be seen as potentially providing a source of income to the North Korean Government. It is currently closed, hopefully temporarily, in response to sanctions on North Korea agreed by the United Nations. At the conclusion of the meeting I was given a bag with some samples of the articles produced, including clothing. My wife Judy examined the label on one article to see how the sensitive question of origin had been handled and whether the label referred to the article being made in South Korea or North Korea or just "Korea". In fact, it read "Made in Peace". This is a suitable aspiration for any business.

References

Annan, K. (1999, January 31). *Address in the World Economic Forum in Davos.* Retrieved from: http://www.unep.fr/shared/publications/other/DTIx0601xPA/pdf/en/delegates/UN_ENVIRO_Del_Mod_1.pdf

Francis I (2015). *Encyclical letter "Laudato Si": On Care for Our Common Home.* Vatican City: Vatican Press. Retrieved from: http://w2.vatican.va/content/francesco/en/encyclicals/documents/papa-francesco_20150524_enciclica-laudato-si.html

Kell, G., Kingo, L., & Reynolds, F. (2015, August 7). *Open Letter to his Holiness Pope Francis from the United Nations Global Compact Responding to Laudato Si.* Retrieved from: https://www.unglobalcompact.org/docs/issues_doc/Environment/Laudato_Si_Open_Letter_UN_Global_Compact.pdf

Moody-Stuart, M. (2014). *Responsible Leadership: Lessons from the Front Line of Sustainability and Ethics.* Sheffield, UK: Greenleaf Publishing.

DOI: [10.9774/GLEAF.4700.2016.de.00006]

Laudato Si

An Environmental Watershed?

Jeffrey Ball
Stanford University, USA

Pope Francis wowed the world last year with his famous encyclical calling for global action on climate change. Since then, he has received visits from eco-minded dignitaries wanting to bask in his glow, been given free electric bikes, and been suggested as a fitting candidate for winner of the Nobel Prize. Whether his encyclical really will do much to curb carbon emissions, however, remains to be seen.

- Encyclical Laudato Si
- Carbon emissions
- Pope Francis
- Climate change

Jeffrey Ball, a writer whose work focuses on energy and the environment, is scholar-in-residence at Stanford University's Steyer-Taylor Center for Energy Policy and Finance and a lecturer at Stanford Law School. His writing appears in a variety of national publications.

jeffball@stanford.edu

N MAY 2015, POPE FRANCIS wowed the world with his famous encyclical calling for urgent action to address the "grave implications" of climate change (Francis, 2015). Since then, he has been visited by actor and eco-activist Leonardo DiCaprio (USA Today, 2016), given free electric bikes by an Italian manufacturer (Agenzia Nationale Stampa Associata, 2016), and floated as a candidate for the Nobel Prize (Christian, 2016). As a popularizer of the message that climate change is a serious problem, the Pope, with a flock of 1 billion Catholics, has no equal. Whether his pronouncement actually will do much to curb carbon emissions remains to be seen.

Climate change is the thorniest of all environmental problems. Its causes are global, meaning they are impossible to blame on any particular company or country, and they are systemic, meaning they are a product of essentially every daily activity in an international economy powered by fossil fuels. The effects of global warming, meanwhile, are long term and tough to see. Contrast that with the environmental ills that the world's most advanced economies have largely solved: smog, water pollution, and buried industrial waste. Those ecological challenges are local, with clearer causes and simpler solutions.

In his 192-page climate encyclical, written with the input of climate scientists and government environmental regulators from around the world, Pope Francis called climate change a frightening sign that things "are now reaching a breaking point" with the environment. He lamented the "regrettably few" serious international efforts to combat global warming, adding: "It is remarkable how weak international political responses have been" (Francis, 2015).

The encyclical, called "Laudato Si: On Care for Our Common Home", was as much an expression of concern about climate change's social implications as about its environmental ones. It blamed climate change mostly on the rich world—on "extreme and selective consumerism on the part of some"—yet it noted that global warming's effects are likely to be felt mostly in poorer countries, whose infrastructure is less able to adapt to changing temperatures (Francis, 2015). In parsing the problem this way—in ascribing it not to population growth but to crass consumption by one slice of the population—the encyclical placed itself firmly in the tradition of prior Catholic teaching. The question it begged is how to deal with the reality that, from now on, virtually all of the increase in global carbon emissions will come from countries that today are developing, not developed.

Unquestionably, the papal call appears to have boosted public concern about climate change. One US nun told me that, in Catholic churches across the country, groups of believers had begun studying the encyclical with an attention to detail and a fervour that they long had reserved for the Bible itself. A report last November by the Yale Project on Climate Change Communication and the George Mason University Center for Climate Change Communication coined a catchy term for the public's reaction to Laudato Si: "The Francis Effect" (Maibach et al., 2015).

The report said that polling both before and after the issuance of Laudato Si showed that the encyclical had significantly amplified public concern about global warming. According to the study, between March 2015 and November 2015, the portions of Americans who believed global warming is happening, is worrisome, and is very or extremely important to them personally all rose—and rose more markedly among Catholics than among Americans as a whole.

And yet, the report's numbers showed, even months after the encyclical was issued, fewer than 30% of Catholics and of Americans thought global warming was very or extremely important to them personally, fewer than half of both groups saw climate change as a moral issue, and fewer than 15% of both groups thought it was a religious issue. More strikingly, the poll by the Yale and George Mason centres found that the number of Americans who say human activity causes global warming changed not at all as a result of the Pope's pronouncement (Maibach et al., 2015). That's a key caveat. If the public doesn't see climate change as linked to human activity, the public is highly unlikely to endorse policies that, in the name of climate change, seek to change the way humans consume energy.

Separate polling by the Pew Research Center similarly shows public reaction to climate change as measured and complex. The report, based on polling Pew did in spring 2015, reports rising public concern but also deep divisions over climate change. Those divisions lay bare how difficult it would be to muster support for the sort of economic actions widely seen as necessary to meaningfully address the problem.

Globally, according to the Pew poll, a median of 54% of people thinks climate change is a very serious problem and a median of 40% is very concerned that climate change will harm them personally. But regionally, the differences in public opinion on these questions are wide, telling and sobering (Stokes et al., 2015).

The extent of concern about climate change is highest in Latin America and Africa—two regions that, broadly speaking, have contributed among the least to worldwide carbon emissions but that face among the greatest potential damage from the effects of climate change. In Latin America, according to the Pew poll, 74% of people think climate change is a very serious problem and 63% are very concerned that it will harm them personally.

In Africa, the poll found, the numbers were 61% on both of those two questions. Contrast that with public opinion in China and the United States, which are, respectively, the world's No. 1 and No. 2 energy consumers and carbon emitters. In the United States, 45% of people see climate change as a very serious problem and 30% are very concerned that climate change will harm them personally. In China, the numbers are 18% and 15%, respectively (Stokes et al., 2015). (China uses more energy and emits more carbon dioxide than the United States even though its economy is smaller. One important reason is that China remains a global factory floor. Much of its economy centres on manufacturing goods that are exported and consumed in other countries, prominent among them the United States.)

The insight from polling that concern about climate change is lower in the countries emitting the greatest amount of carbon dioxide goes a long way towards explaining why Laudato Si, despite its lofty language, hasn't translated into sweeping climate action. In December 2015, diplomats from around the world met for a global climate conference in Paris, a gathering billed by boosters as one of the world's last opportunities to agree to cut carbon emissions on the scale that most scientists say would be necessary to avoid dangerous consequences from global warming. Politically, the Paris conference succeeded. Dozens of countries, both developed and developing, ponied up promises to curb their carbon outputs, allowing diplomats to call the Paris agreement, accurately, the first truly global climate accord. But practically, the Paris conference amounted to only a tiny step. Study after study has concluded that the promises proffered in Paris by all those countries add up to nowhere near enough reductions in carbon emissions to prevent average global temperatures from surpassing 2 degrees Celsius above pre-industrial levels (Ball, 2015). That is the threshold that most scientists have identified as important for the planet not to cross (UNFCCC, 2010).

Pope Francis's climate encyclical was everywhere on the lips of the negotiators in Paris. But for Laudato Si to prove an environmental watershed rather than a mere rhetorical device, it will have to move more than hearts, more than minds, and more than lips. It will have to move the global economy—a system built for decades on the consumption of cheap and convenient coal, oil and natural gas. At issue is shifting personal behaviour, economic policies and trillions of dollars.

References

Agenzia Nazionale Stampa Associata (2016, January 27). Pope given 10 electric bikes to thank him for encyclical. *ANSA*. Retrieved from: http://www.ansa.it/english/news/2016/01/27/pope-given-10-electric-bikes-to-thank-him-for-encyclical_20d5df93-61fe-4ddf-ac7c-3e7244d6e3f3.html

Ball, J. (2015, December 12). The Paris climate conference deal is a step forward. Even if only a small one. *New Republic*. Retrieved from: https://newrepublic.com/article/125690/paris-climate-conference-deal-step-forward

Christian, R. (2016, February 26). Pope Francis should win this year's Nobel Peace Prize. *National Catholic Reporter*. Retrieved from: https://www.ncronline.org/blogs/distinctly-catholic/pope-francis-should-win-year-s-nobel-peace-prize

Francis I (2015). *Encyclical letter "Laudato Si": On Care for Our Common Home*. Vatican City: Vatican Press. Retrieved from: http://w2.vatican.va/content/francesco/en/encyclicals/documents/papa-francesco_20150524_enciclica-laudato-si.html

Maibach, E., Leiserowitz, A., Roser-Renouf, C., Myers, T., Rosenthal, S., & Feinberg, G. (2015). *The Francis Effect: How Pope Francis Changed the Conversation about Global Warming*. Fairfax, VA: George Mason University Center for Climate Change Communication. Retrieved from: http://climatecommunication.yale.edu/publications/the-francis-effect/

Stokes, B., Wike, R., & Carle, J. (2015, November 5). Global concern about climate change, broad support for limiting emissions: U.S., China less worried; Partisan divides in key countries. *Pew Research Center*. Retrieved from: http://www.pewglobal.org/2015/11/05/global-concern-about-climate-change-broad-support-for-limiting-emissions/

UNFCCC (2010, March 30). *Report of the Conference of the Parties on its Fifteenth session, Held in Copenhagen from 7 to 19 December 2009*. Retrieved from: http://unfccc.int/resource/docs/2009/cop15/eng/11a01.pdf

USA Today (2016, January 28). Leonardo DiCaprio meets with Pope Francis. *USA Today*. Retrieved from: http://www.usatoday.com/story/life/movies/2016/01/28/oscar-hopeful-dicaprio-huddles-pope-francis-vatican/79454458/

DOI: [10.9774/GLEAF.4700.2016.de.00007]

The 3M Company

Applying the Theory and Changing the World

Jean Bennington Sweeney

3M, USA

3M believes industry holds the key to addressing the issues represented by the UN Global Compact Principles and the 2030 Sustainable Development Goals. Our brand "3M Science.Applied to Life". clearly commits us to helping solve these intractable challenges, and partnering with our communities, customers and other stakeholders to amplify our efforts. Through our operations, our products and our inspiration, 3M is proud to be positively and sustainably contributing to the betterment of our society, and yet we recognize there is still much left to do. The UNGC Principles and the SDGs provide a shared vision to which 3M has been aligned and working towards for decades ... one where we can all strive to improve our businesses, our planet and every life.

● 3M
● Sustainability
● United Nations Global Compact
● UNGC
● Sustainable Development Goals
● SDGs

Jean Bennington Sweeney, is Chief Sustainability Officer for 3M Company. She has held a diversity of positions at 3M in product development, manufacturing and business management including an operations assignment in 3M Australia and managing director of 3M Taiwan. In her current role, she is responsible for 3M environment, health, safety and sustainability programmes globally. Jean holds a degree in chemical engineering from Montana State University and an MBA from the University of St Thomas, St Paul, Minnesota.

jbsweeney@mmm.com

Who we are and what we stand for

At 3M, it is our view that real change begins with a clearly defined purpose. Through specifically defined goals that come from the highest levels of leadership, we are able to make substantive changes throughout our business and our communities. We hold that a commitment to sustainability and improving everyday life must inform how we approach every idea, every product and every individual. That commitment is born out of Our Brand: "3M Science. Applied to Life". (3M, 2016, *3M Story*).

With worldwide global sales of US$30 billion annually and operations in 70 countries, 3M is intricately woven into the global economy and deeply invested in humanity and its various communities (3M, 2016, *3M Facts, Year-end 2015*). Our industries range from consumer to healthcare to electronics to automotive, so it is important that we take all possible efforts to make daily life easier, safer and more fulfilling. Sustainability is embedded in Our Vision, and Our Vision was created to promote the good 3M can do for people everywhere:

> 3M Technology Advancing Every Company
> 3M Products Enhancing Every Home
> 3M Innovation Improving Every Life

Specifically, Our Brand and Our Vision mean that science is just science unless you make it do something, change something, improve something. Our products and scientific research continually impact people's everyday lives and we want to ensure they do more than just make a business impact on the world—we want to ensure that our technologies and products make the world a better place. The right science applied the right way helps improve the environment and generates breakthroughs that make life better and easier around the globe. These concepts are at the heart of how we integrate corporate citizenship theory into practice every day.

Since our ambition is to apply 3M innovation to improve every life, our long-standing leadership in environmental stewardship and commitment to customer-inspired innovation must be constantly strengthened. 3M has a wide variety of resources and employees, so we are in a unique position to help create a more sustainable future. Today, we use Our Vision as a blueprint for our sustainability strategy on overcoming the global challenges that serve as barriers to improving every life. This means using our greatest assets—ideas and innovation—to address the challenges laid out by the United Nations Sustainable Development Goals (SDGs) and our own 3M Sustainability Goals.

Because of the diversity of our company, we take great efforts to ensure that our scientists, engineers, marketers and sales people work together with customers, suppliers, academics and governments to develop the best strategies for improving lives. We are continually developing new technologies that improve discussions and feedback with our customers and our partners to solve problems around the world. We are more than just a vehicle for profit; we are committed to improving the world as well as growing our business, and we recognize that business and industry must take a leadership role to address the world's most intractable challenges. Sustainability has always been a core value at 3M, and we continue to seek opportunities to act on it.

3M's commitment to human rights, labour, environment and anti-corruption

In February of 2014, 3M became a signatory to the United Nations Global Compact (UNGC) (3M, 2016, *3M and The UNGC*). We committed to aligning our operations and strategies with their ten universally accepted principles in the areas of human rights, labour, environment and anti-corruption. Through this commitment, we expressed our dedication to making the Principles part of the culture and day-to-day operations of our company. We also sought opportunities to advance the broad application of the United Nations goals around the world.

Although we recently became a signatory to the UNGC, 3M has always strived to act in line with the core values represented by the UNGC since its inception. For more than a century, 3M has been a strong supporter of human rights and fair labour practices around the world. Prior to joining the UNGC, we issued a strong Human Rights Policy Statement (3M, 2016, May 1), which expresses our commitment to fighting forced labour, child labour and discrimination of any kind in our workplace. We also have a history of supporting the right of our employees to decide whether or not to join a union.

Our commitment to environmental responsibility (3M, 2015) significantly pre-dates our membership with the UNGC. In 1975, Dr Joseph Ling, 3M's first Vice President of Environment, established the Pollution Prevention Pays (3P) programme, which celebrated its 40th anniversary in 2015. This grass-roots programme depends on 3M employees all over the world to identify and implement projects that not only reduce emissions, waste, and water or energy usage, but also save money. In the past 40 years, 3M employees have implemented over 12,000 3P projects that have prevented over 1.8 million tonnes of pollution (3M, 2016, *2016 Sustainability Report*, p. 67).

We set our first environmental footprint reduction targets in 1990 (3M, 2016, *2016 Sustainability Report*, p. 8). A strong part of our company history, these goals have helped dramatically reduce our environmental footprint and established us as a leader in environmental stewardship. 3M has also provided ongoing support to protect and restore vital ecosystems around the world. By working with partners such as The Nature Conservancy, the 3M Foundation has provided more than US$21 million to preserve more than 400,000 hectares of natural forest (The Nature Conservancy, 2016).

3M has always demanded the highest standards of ethics and integrity from our employees throughout the world. Our Code of Conduct (3M, 2016, 3M Code of Conduct) serves as the foundation for our ethics and compliance programme and instructs our employees to be good, be honest, be fair and impartial, be loyal, be accurate and be respectful. Be Honest requires our employees and business partners to act with transparency and integrity in the global marketplace. 3M has no tolerance for corruption and for violations of the principles of fair competition. Be Respectful calls on all 3M employees to treat each other, the communities where we live and work, and our physical environment with dignity and value. Our global culture of compliance is supported through systems and processes that have been developed to monitor the programme and our improvement efforts.

We are continually recognized for our commitment to the highest levels of integrity and ethics. In 2016, 3M was honoured as a World's Most Ethical Company® by Ethisphere for the third consecutive year (The Ethisphere Institute, 2016).

We also take our role in helping to advance sustainability within our "sphere of influence"—as the UNGC refers to it—very seriously. Our Supplier Responsibility Code (3M, 2016, *3M Supplier Responsibility Code*) holds all companies from whom we purchase materials or services to the same high standards as we have for ourselves, including to the UNGC Principles. We regularly review our operations—and those of our suppliers—to make sure they align with our principles. Each 3M operation, everywhere in the world, is responsible for putting these principles and commitments in practice in their facility.

3M's 2025 Sustainability Goals and the SDGs

Our 2025 Sustainability Goals were created collaboratively based on extensive internal and external stakeholder research. The goals were finalized and announced in spring 2015 (3M, 2015). Our current goals are the broadest and most global they have ever been, with an increased emphasis on positive social impacts. Figure 1 provides a quick thumbnail of our 2025 goals with respect to the five global challenges most material to 3M: raw materials; water; energy and climate; health & safety; and education and development.

Figure 1 3M's 2025 Sustainability Goals
Source: 3M (2015)

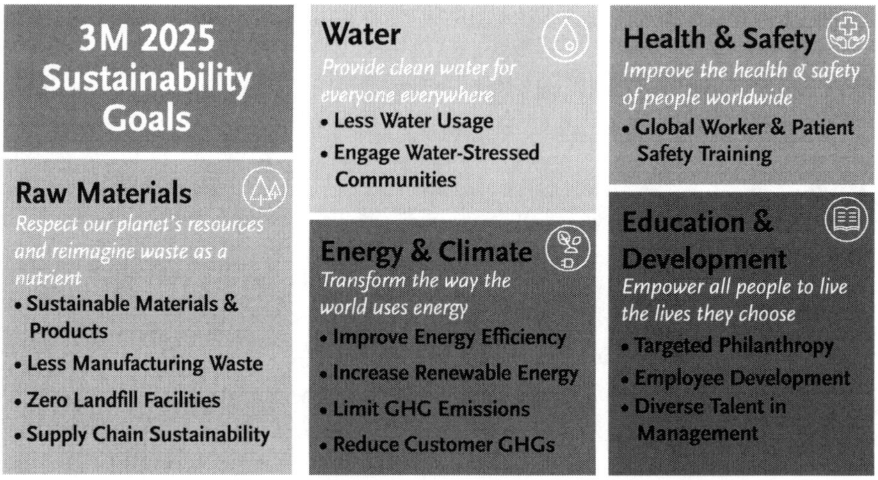

3M 2025 Sustainability Goals

Water
Provide clean water for everyone everywhere
- Less Water Usage
- Engage Water-Stressed Communities

Health & Safety
Improve the health & safety of people worldwide
- Global Worker & Patient Safety Training

Raw Materials
Respect our planet's resources and reimagine waste as a nutrient
- Sustainable Materials & Products
- Less Manufacturing Waste
- Zero Landfill Facilities
- Supply Chain Sustainability

Energy & Climate
Transform the way the world uses energy
- Improve Energy Efficiency
- Increase Renewable Energy
- Limit GHG Emissions
- Reduce Customer GHGs

Education & Development
Empower all people to live the lives they choose
- Targeted Philanthropy
- Employee Development
- Diverse Talent in Management

It is easy to see how well aligned the 3M Sustainability Goals are with the United Nations Sustainable Development Goals (3M, 2016, March 11), shown in Figure 2. We are both focused on overcoming the global challenges that serve as barriers to improving every life.

Figure 2 United Nations Sustainable Development Goals
Source: http://www.globalgoals.org/

Raw materials

We recognize that our planet has limited resources, and we want to ensure that future generations will have similar access to the materials they need to thrive. Thus, we aim to view waste as a nutrient that through technology and corporate strategy can be reused and sustained. This aligns with the United Nations Sustainable Development Goal Number 12: "Ensure sustainable consumption and production patterns".

The 3M goal to "invest to develop more sustainable materials and products to help our customers reach their environmental goals" recognizes that one of the best ways to amplify our impact is to help customers improve their environmental footprint.

One example of this goal in action is 3M's Thermal Bonding Films and Plastics Bonding Adhesives, which extend the potential lifespan of mobile devices and make it easier to recycle them. Our electronics bonding solutions enable faster assembly times and simplify rework by helping manufacturers fix damaged parts and salvage key components (3M, 2016, *2016 Sustainability Report*, p. 73).

Our other raw material goals are focused on continuing to improve our own performance: reduce manufacturing waste by an additional 10% (indexed to sales); and achieve "zero landfill" status at more than 30% of manufacturing sites. To reduce waste, we are focused on rethinking product designs and process technologies to eliminate waste before it is generated, as well as repurposing,

reusing and recycling potential waste materials at our manufacturing operations via our Pollution Prevention Pays (3P) programme.

Our final Raw Materials 2025 Sustainability Goal is to "drive supply chain sustainability through targeted raw material traceability and supplier performance
assurance". To drive environmental and social expectations of our suppliers, we
are using a comprehensive risk-based approach to engage critical supply chains
for collaboration and improvement.

One important commodity area where 3M requires specific sustainability
performance from our suppliers is for paper-based materials. The 3M Pulp and
Paper Sourcing Policy (3M, 2013) formalizes our commitment to ensuring our
forest materials supply chains practise compliant, responsible and sustainable
forestry. We implement this policy with a 5-step Due Diligence Management
System, modelled after guidance from the Organization for Economic Cooperation and Development (OECD, 2016), and we encourage our suppliers
to do the same. This work directly aligns with United Nations Sustainable
Development Goal Number 15 (among others): "Protect, restore and promote
sustainable use of terrestrial ecosystems, sustainably manage forests, combat
desertification, and halt and reverse land degradation and halt biodiversity loss".
Forests play a critical role in combating climate change, supporting water quality and biodiversity, and providing community and cultural significance. We
are committed to doing our part to ensure the health and abundance of these
critical natural resources.

Water

Our 2025 goals are also focused on promoting clean water for every person
around the globe to help promote better lives, businesses and communities. Our
goal to "reduce global water use by an additional 10%, indexed to sales" focuses
on our operations' water impacts. Our goal to "engage 100% of water-stressed/
scarce communities where 3M manufactures on community-wide approaches
to water management" expands our impact beyond our operations, into the
communities in which we live and work. 3M's water-related goals align closely
with the United Nations Sustainable Development Goal Number 6: "Ensure
availability and sustainable management of water and sanitation for all".

Building upon our previous 42% reduction in water usage between 2005
and 2014 (3M, 2016, 2016 Sustainability Report, p. 13), we will continue to drive
water reduction conservation processes and technology changes within our
operations with a "respect every drop" mind-set. By partnering with local communities to advance water recycling and conservation, we seek to help these
communities build and manage their own efforts toward access to clean water
into the future.

3M is well positioned to help communities reliably provide clean water. We
created 3M™ Scotchkote™ water pipe coatings and linings to help customers
protect water quality and reduce losses from water main deterioration (3M,
2016, 3M™ Scotchkote™ Pipe Renewal). These types of products help assure

communities all over the world that they will have clean, safe water to use in their homes and businesses.

We are also actively working to ensure responsible water usage in our factories around the world. For example, the 3M plant in Sumare, Brazil has a history of water reuse actions focused on self-sufficiency, sustainability and preservation of the environment. Recent projects, including wastewater recycling and reuse, have resulted in an overall decrease of the plant's water usage indexed to output by over 45%. 3M Sumare shares the knowledge gained through its actions with other local companies interested in improving their water efficiency.

Climate and energy

Climate change is one of the world's most complex and urgent challenges, and industry plays a critical role in addressing it. 3M's goals on climate and energy are aligned with the United Nations Sustainable Goal Number 13: "Take urgent action to combat climate change and its impacts".

► Ensure greenhouse gas (GHG) emissions at least 50% below our 2002 baseline, while growing our business

► Help our customers reduce their GHGs by 250 million tons of CO_2 equivalent emissions through use of 3M products

► Improve energy efficiency indexed to net sales by 30%

► Increase renewable energy to 25% of total electricity use

3M is in a leadership position due to our early actions to reduce our greenhouse gas emissions beginning more than 10 years ago. Between 2002 and 2015, we voluntarily achieved a 69% absolute reduction in greenhouse gas emissions (3M, 2016, *2016 Sustainability Report*, p. 13). While 3M has made significant GHG emission reductions across our global operations, we realize we can make far greater contributions by helping our customers reduce their GHG emissions through the use of our products, so that will be our main focus.

A hallmark example of a 3M product that fights against rising greenhouse gas emissions is 3M Novec Engineered Fluids. This is a revolutionary two-phase immersion cooling technology which can reduce cooling energy usage in data centres by 95%, slashing GHG emissions in the process (3M, 2015, March 13). We are committed to increasing the use of this and other GHG-saving products around the world.

Building on our 50% improvement in energy efficiency between 2000 and 2014, a 30% energy efficiency improvement will keep our global energy use nearly flat over the next 10 years, even as the company grows. Across the globe, nearly 800,000 MWh of renewable energy use will be added, primarily through wind and solar projects (3M, 2016, *2016 Sustainability Report*, p. 86).

Health & Safety

Our 2025 Sustainability Goal around health & safety is to "provide training to 5 million people globally on worker and patient safety". We recognize that proper use of health and safety products is critical to infection prevention, personal safety, and overall health. We feel we have a responsibility to share our expertise in healthcare safety and personal protective equipment like respirators and fall protection with as much of the world as possible. Building on our existing customer education programme, we seek to help educate individuals on worker and patient safety in both healthcare and industrial settings. This goal aligns closely with the United Nations Sustainable Development Goal Number 3: "Ensure healthy lives and promote well-being for all at all ages".

Nearly 45 years ago, 3M introduced the first in a long line of National Institute for Occupational Safety and Health (NIOSH) approved respirators for a variety of industries from agriculture to healthcare to construction and more (3M, 2016, *Worker Health and Safety*). Over the years our technologies have improved, our methodologies have changed and our research has led to industry breakthroughs. 3M is partnering with other industries, governments and organizations to improve access to life-saving equipment and education for farmers, miners, healthcare professionals and everyday citizens in communities around the world.

Education and development

Finally, we have three 2025 Sustainability Goals surrounding education and development, which align with, among others, the United Nations Sustainable Development Goal Number 4: "Ensure inclusive and equitable quality education and promote lifelong learning opportunities for all" and Number 5: "Achieve gender equality and empower all women and girls".

▶ Invest cash and products for education, community and environmental programmes

▶ 100% participation in employee development programmes to advance individual and organizational capabilities

▶ Double the pipeline of diverse talent in management to build a diverse workforce

Last year 3M invested more than $70 million in cash and in-kind donations to support global educational, community and environmental initiatives. These donations were bolstered by the more than 300,000 volunteer hours from 3M employees and retirees around the world (3M, 2016, *2016 Sustainability Report*, p. 123).

In 2014, we launched the 3M Global Volunteer Day, with a theme of mentoring students or youth or supporting organizations that serve them. In 2015 that event involved over 16,000 volunteers in 88 countries serving in schools and youth organizations from St Paul to Spain to South Africa (3M, 2016, *2016*

Sustainability Report, pp. 50-53). These various programmes are designed to ensure healthy lives, promote the wellbeing of people of all ages and promote lifelong learning, just as the UNGC goals promote.

Conclusion

The United Nations Sustainable Development Goals are a positive step forward that all businesses should be striving toward. 3M's 2025 Goals were developed to both align with those of the UNGC and continue 3M's storied commitment to improving the world for all people. 3M believes these goals are furthered by working closely with our customers, suppliers and partners to create the best possible outcomes. By clearly defining these goals at the highest levels of 3M, we are expressing to our employees the importance of driving transformational change through innovation.

3M has shown a strong commitment to the areas of human rights, labour, environment and anti-corruption since its inception. Our aim to make the world a better place is not merely aspirational—we take active steps to make it a reality, as evidenced by our 2025 Sustainability Goals and our partnership with the UNGC.

We recognize that strong partnerships and clearly defined goals are essential to creating real, positive change. In addition to partnering with the UNGC, 3M recently partnered with Nobel Media in March 2016 (3M, 2016, March 11). This international partnership brings together two respected organizations committed to the advancement of innovation, education and scientific research. As one of a select group of partners, 3M will collaborate with Nobel Media over several years to bring to light important global issues, such as the future of scientific education and sustainability.

In conclusion, 3M recognizes that creating long-term, positive changes to the environment and for everyday people is not easy. It requires continual shifts in how we operate, how we make long-term decisions and how we collaborate. We are proud to partner with the United Nations, UNGC signatories and responsible businesses everywhere because these partnerships are more than just words and aspirations—they represent specifically defined goals and actions that turn the theory of corporate citizenship into actions that create stronger businesses and a better world for all of us.

References

3M (2013). *3M Sourcing Policy: Pulp and Paper Sourcing Policy*. Retrieved from: http://multimedia.3m.com/mws/media/1033586O/pulp-and-paper-policy.pdf?fn=Pulp%20and%20Paper%20Sourcing%20Policy%20M

3M (2013, May 1). *Human Rights Policy*. Retrieved from: http://multimedia.3m.com/mws/media/1029705O/human-rights-policy-statement.pdf

3M (2014). *Environmental, Health and Safety Policy*. Retrieved from: http://multimedia.3m.com/mws/media/1029685O/environmental-policy.pdf

3M (2015). *2015 Sustainability Report Executive Summary*. Retrieved from: http://multimedia.3m.com/mws/media/1090359O/3m-2015-sustainability-report-executive-summary.pdf

3M (2015, March 13). *How less creates more in hardware cooling*. Retrieved from: http://www.3m.com/3M/en_US/sustainability-us/stories/full-story/?storyid=24f1f168-d611-4004-b321-279e7056961b

3M (2016). *2016 Sustainability Report*. Retrieved from: http://multimedia.3m.com/mws/media/1214315O/2016-3m-sustainability-report.pdf

3M (2016). *3M and the UNGC*. Retrieved from: http://www.3m.com/3M/en_US/sustainability-us/policies-reports/global-compact/

3M (2016). *3M Code of Conduct*. Retrieved from: http://solutions.3m.com/wps/portal/3M/en_US/businessconduct/bcmain/

3M (2016). *3M Facts, Year-end 2015*. Retrieved from: http://multimedia.3m.com/mws/media/496996O/3m-facts.pdf

3M (2016). *3M™ Scotchkote™ Pipe Renewal*. Retrieved from: http://www.3m.com/3M/en_US/company-us/all-3m-products/~/3M-Scotchkote-Pipe-Renewal-Liner-2400?N=5002385+8709322+8709409+8710650+8710719+8711017+8711732+3294742899&rt=rud

3M (2016). *3M Story*. Retrieved from: http://www.3m.com/3M/en_US/company-us/3m-science-applied-to-life/

3M (2016). *3M Supplier Responsibility Code*. Retrieved from: http://multimedia.3m.com/mws/media/1204567O/3m-supplier-responsibility-code.pdf

3M (2016). *Worker Health and Safety*. Retrieved from: http://www.3m.com/3M/en_US/worker-health-safety-us/safety-resources-training-news/calendar-of-events/n95/?WT.mc_id=www.3m.com/n95

3M (2016, March 11). *3M and Nobel Media Partnership*. Retrieved from: http://news.3m.com/press-release/company-english/3m-and-nobel-media-announce-international-partnership

3M (2016, March 11). *3M and United Nations' 2030 Agenda for Sustainable Development*. Retrieved from: http://www.3m.com/3M/en_US/sustainability-us/stories/full-story/?storyid=6ede4528-b5c3-441c-b204-5e8b7425d3be

Global Goals (2016). *The Global Goals for Sustainable Development*. Retrieved from: http://www.globalgoals.org/

OECD (2016). *OECD Due Diligence Guidance for Responsible Supply Chains of Minerals from Conflict-Affected and High-Risk Areas* (3rd ed.). Retrieved from: http://www.oecd.org/daf/inv/mne/mining.htm

The Ethisphere Institute (2016). *Homepage*. Retrieved from: http://worldsmostethicalcompanies.ethisphere.com/

The Nature Conservancy (2016). *Companies We Work With*. Retrieved from: http://www.nature.org/about-us/working-with-companies/companies-we-work-with/3m.xml

DOI: [10.9774/GLEAF.4700.2016.de.00008]

Pope Francis and the United Nations

Planet Partners

Gerald F. Cavanagh
University of Detroit Mercy, USA

Pope Francis's Encyclical letter "Care for Our Common Home" ["Laudato Si"] summons all to better care for the planet and for poor peoples. Francis discusses the same challenges as do the United Nations Sustainable Development Goals. In this paper I compare the two statements, focusing more on Care for Our Common Home, while also examining the contributions and criticisms of the document. Francis describes how we wastefully use our resources and trash our planet. He explains how selfishness and financial gain often prevail over human dignity and the natural environment, and how the poor suffer the most from our self-centred actions. Francis says we urgently need a broadened, humanistic vision that reflects the needs of others, especially the poor and future generations who are most at risk.

- Pope Francis
- United Nations Sustainable Development Goals
- Sustainability
- UNGC
- Care for Our Common Home
- Laudato Si

Gerald (Jerry) Cavanagh is the Fisher Chair of Business Ethics and Professor of Management at the University of Detroit Mercy. He has authored 40 research articles and five books; the latest book is American Business Values: A Global Perspective. Jerry Cavanagh has lectured on business ethics throughout the US, as well as in Mexico, Indonesia, Australia, Europe and India. A Jesuit Catholic priest, he holds a B.S. in engineering and graduate degrees in philosophy, theology, education, and a doctorate in management. He was Provost at the University of Detroit Mercy and Interim Dean at the College of Business Administration. He has also held the Gasson Chair at Boston College and the Dirksen Chair of Business Ethics at the Santa Clara University. He chaired the Social Issues Division of the Academy of Management, and the All-Academy of Management Task Force on Ethics.

✉ University of Detroit Mercy,
4001 W. McNichols,
Detroit, MI48221-3038,USA

🖥 cavanagf@udmercy.edu

POPE FRANCIS AND THE UNITED Nations have parallel agendas. I examine Francis's Encyclical, "Care for Our Common Home" ["Laudato Si" or "Praise Be to You"], describe the contributions of the document and also present some of the criticisms of it. I will also show some similarities and contrasts between it and the United Nations Sustainable Development Goals. Both documents are the result of extensive consultation and discussion with many diverse stakeholders. The content of each covers many of the same global issues. However, the style of the two documents differs markedly.

The United Nations Sustainable Development Goals (UN, 2015) are clear, straightforward goals with detailed sub-goals that require each of the 195 nations which signed the goals to implement them in their own countries. Care for Our Common Home (Francis, 2015) is an engaging, comprehensive, principled exhortation in six chapters that is directed to Catholic Christians and also to all conscientious, individual citizens and national leaders. It seeks to present a moral claim on our conscience, and it calls for specific actions. It came as a surprise to many that Pope Francis's Care for Our Common Home received more global attention than have the United Nations Sustainable Development Goals. Table 1 provides a brief summary comparison of the two statements.

Table 1 Summary comparison of: Care for Our Common Home and the United Nations 17 Principles for Sustainable Development

	Pope Francis: Care for Our Common Home	United Nations 17 Principles for Sustainable Development
Goal	Keep planet healthy and help poor peoples: integral ecology	Keep planet healthy, help poor peoples, plus more specific goals
Target audience	All persons and leaders of nations	All persons and leaders of nations
Source of statement	Pope Francis and Catholic traditions	Agreement of world leaders
Rationale for urging action	Moral responsibility to help the poor and hand on a habitable planet	Global strategic need, plus political and scientific consensus
Moral foundation for statement	Social justice principles and Sacred Scriptures	Social justice and consensus
Credibility of statement	Francis "walks his talk" on environment and care for poor	Some leaders of nations do not act on the 17 Principles
Style of document	Engaging, accessible, easy to read exhortation	Straightforward, fact-based, well organized
Impact of statement	Extensive initial attention and earlyimpact; uncertain long-term impact	Some initial attention; uncertain long-term impact

Overview of major themes of Francis's encyclical letter

In Chapter One of Pope Francis's letter, "What is Happening to our Common Home" (LS, 17-61) (the numbers refer to the paragraphs as they are listed in the Encyclical), Francis presents evidence on the damage to our planet and people: pollution, trash, climate change, shortage of drinkable water, loss of biodiversity, excessive use of fossil fuels and other materials, and the inequality of opportunity among peoples. Francis cites specific examples of our wasteful and damaging actions, ranging from financial speculation to the excessive use of air conditioning. He demonstrates how such actions fail to consider their negative impact on others and the common good. He says that these problems are largely the result of the activities of wealthier nations and corporations, while the poor disproportionately suffer the subsequent harm. Because of this, Francis speaks of a resulting "ecological debt" between the wealthy global north and poorer global south (LS, 51). Francis lists some environmental efforts that have produced positive results, but he also outlines serious dangers, including even the possibility of new wars over scarce resources and land under "the guise of noble claims" (LS, 57-58).

Francis says in Chapter Two, "The Gospel of Creation" (LS, 62-100), that the Bible teaches a harmony between the creator, peoples and all creatures. Yet he charges that because of our individualism and "me-first" mentality, we often arrogantly "take the place of God" and refuse to acknowledge our limitations as creatures. He then restates that "We are not God" (LS, 66-67), and he calls us to recognize the common good.

In Chapter Three, "The Human Roots of the Ecological Crisis" (LS, 101-136), Francis speaks of the "technocratic paradigm" which makes it "easy to accept the idea of infinite or unlimited growth". But this is "based on the lie that there is an infinite supply of the earth's goods". (LS, 106) This same mentality seeks individual technical solutions to each environmental problem, which does not recognize "integral ecology", such that the environment and people are intimately connected. Hence Francis argues for a "less polluting means of production" and "a non-consumerist model of life, recreation and community" (LS, 112). He charges that we suffer from what he calls "anthropocentrism" by which we humans "give absolute priority to immediate convenience and all else becomes relative" (LS, 122). Such relativism "drives one person to take advantage of another, to treat others as mere objects ..." (LS, 123). Francis then speaks of the need for employment, outlines some suggestions for work, and points to "business as a noble vocation ..." that helps to accomplish this (LS, 124-129).

Francis, in Chapter Four, "Integral Ecology" (LS, 137-162), returns to his theme that "we are faced not with separate crises, one environmental and the other social, but rather with one complex crisis which is both social and environmental". Thus solutions "demand an integrated approach to combating poverty, restoring dignity to the excluded, and at the same time protecting nature" (LS, 139). To achieve this, Francis calls on researchers in various disciplines to help develop an "economic ecology" and "a humanism capable of bringing together the different fields of knowledge, including economics, in the service of a more integral and integrating vision" (LS, 141). He then speaks of specific challenges of poverty, overcrowding and lack of open spaces, and the importance of public transportation. To coming generations we are likely leaving debris, desolation and filth (LS, 161). He says that regulations will be effective only if individuals' actions are motivated by a new vision, a new humanism, "integral ecology and an understanding of the common good". He makes the sobering observation that "Doomsday predictions can no longer be met with irony or disdain" (LS, 161).

Chapter Five, "Lines of Approach and Action" (LS, 163-201), emphasizes our interdependence and asks what actions we must take. Francis urges informed, transparent, global dialogue such that actions serve not the economic interests of the financially or politically powerful, but benefit all persons (LS, 164). He points to some environmental successes in global agreements, such as accords to protect the ozone layer and endangered species (LS, 168). But he also notes that individual nation-states are losing power and influence to global financial and economic interests (LS, 175). Even more fundamentally, Francis asks us to redefine what we mean by progress: a "development" "which does not leave in its wake a better world and an integrally higher quality of life cannot be considered progress". He notes that "frequently people's quality of life diminishes—by the deterioration of the environment, the low quality of food or the depletion of resources—in the midst of economic growth" (LS, 194). Francis points out how planning by developed world nations and mechanized farming in developing countries increases the gap between rich and poor, and often makes food more expensive for the poor. Social justice demands that meagre incomes must increase so food is more available to the poor (Rieff, 2015).

In the Sixth and final chapter, "Ecological Education and Spirituality" (LS, 201-246), Francis challenges us to shift to a new lifestyle. He notes that currently many of us are victims of what he calls compulsive consumerism. "The emptier a person's heart is, the more he or she needs things to buy, own and consume" (LS, 204). He emphasizes that "purchasing is always a moral—and not simply economic—act" (LS, 206). He even provides simple suggestions of what each person can do, such as "avoiding the use of plastic and paper, reducing water consumption, separating refuse ... using public transport or car-pooling ..." and more (LS, 211). Francis acknowledges that these actions will not save the world, but he says they liberate the spirit. And he points to the Bible and other religious traditions which teach that "less is more" (LS, 223). In his section on civic and political love, Francis says that we must "regain the conviction that we need one another, that we have a shared responsibility for others and the world, and that being good and decent is worth it" (LS, 229). He finishes his letter by urging us to love and pray for one another.

Contributions of Care for Our Common Home

Urgent issues: environment and poverty

Pope Francis's first encyclical letter addresses some of the most serious issues that face the people of this planet: the rapidly deteriorating natural environment and the dire poverty of so many of the earth's peoples. His central point is that men and women are not separate from the natural environment. We are one with it, and he calls this "integral ecology". He takes a strong position on the importance of quickly confronting global climate change, and he released his letter strategically, prior to the UN climate negotiations in Paris, with the intention of encouraging the participating nations and their leaders to come to an agreement.

Francis's contribution is that he approaches these global challenges as inter-related moral issues (Incropera, 2015). He says that we have a moral obligation to reverse climate change, reduce our waste and unnecessary use of resources, and help persons who are on the margins of society with education, food and, most importantly, employment. While citing the Bible, he notes that the same caring attitudes toward our natural world and the poor are present in other religious traditions, also. Francis provides a new, and for many a more compelling, motivation for action. He insists that supporting our natural environment and poor peoples is a moral obligation for all.

Moral issues

Technology and capitalism falsely promise unlimited growth, according to Francis. He says that we habitually have a blind faith that technology and the free market will solve our problems (LS, 102-111). However, while money is made, in doing so we have degraded our planet and only a small minority of very wealthy people receive most of the financial rewards. Francis condemns "practical relativism" and self-seeking individualism, which motivates our blind faith in the market and technology (LS, 122-123). Self-interest as a predominant motivation characterizes a person who is less morally developed (Kohlberg, 1978; Damon, 1999). Francis contrasts such individualism with a more morally developed attitude toward people which is rooted in respect for the human dignity of all, the common good and care for the natural world. He says that our ecological crises are a consequence of the ethical, cultural and spiritual crises of our modern world. He condemns what he calls the "technocratic paradigm" (LS, 106) and "anthropocentrism" (LS, 115).

On the individual level, Francis points out how marketing and advertising encourage us to purchase, so "people can easily get caught up in a whirlwind of needless buying and spending". He calls this "compulsive consumerism", which is rooted in "me-first", wasteful habits. From his moral, ethical and spiritual platform, Francis cites indifference, selfishness and greed as the root of these problems (LS, 203-204). For each of us, Francis favourably refers to the traditional, but now ironically countercultural, Christian position that "less is more" with regards to what we own and what we purchase (Mahoney, 2015).

Francis calls all to a global dialogue on these issues. He urges people of all nations and faiths to review the facts and then confront the challenges with local and regional actions. But he understands that a consensus among nations and peoples is needed to achieve "enforceable international agreements" (LS, 173-175).

Wide consultation

As a part of preparation and consultation for the encyclical, Francis organized a workshop of leading scholars and global climate scientists. He met with them to hear their scientific findings and obtain their advice for the letter. As a result, Francis is praised by leaders of the US and international scientific community for obtaining the best advice available before writing the letter. The Vatican organized the preparatory workshop and in the words of the editor of the prestigious journal, *Science*, who was present and presented a paper at the consultation, "the attendees included Hindus, Muslims, Protestants, Jews, atheists, and agnostics, all willing to follow this leader, not because of his religious significance, but because of his moral high ground" (McNutt, 2015) . Additional scientists attended the Vatican dialogue and also praised and supported the content of the encyclical (Dasgupta and Ramanathan, 2015), and similar support was voiced in an editorial in the scientific journal, *Nature* (2015).

Writing style of encyclical

Francis's writing style is clear, direct and engaging. Previous Papal Encyclicals were often largely abstract theology, and many people find them difficult to read. Francis uses graphic language and provides specific examples and recommendations. He writes the letter to all people of all faiths worldwide. Thus the letter is translated into many languages.

The encyclical received considerable public attention for several reasons. It is, of course, on issues of enormous importance to the peoples and nations of the world. It is written by a person with considerable moral and personal authority. And it is engaging and understandable. In addition, Francis reinforced his message when he spoke several months later to the US Congress and to the United Nations.

Personal lifestyle

Francis not only urges actions by individuals, nations and international groups, but he lives according to his own message. He resides in a small room in the Vatican guest centre, Domus Sanctae Marthae, rather than in the traditional, regal Papal Apartments. He travels in a small, fuel efficient car, and as a bishop and cardinal in Argentina, he travelled on buses and the subway. After he was elected pope, he paid his own bill at the hotel where he was staying and he himself cancelled his newspaper subscriptions in Buenos Aires. He visits prisoners, poor people, refugees and persons with disabilities, and he does this regularly in place of elaborate dinners with presidents and kings. On Good Friday, Francis was pictured on the front page of the *Wall Street Journal* at a shelter near Rome washing and kissing the feet of Muslim, Hindu and Christian refugees (*Wall Street Journal*, 2016). He consistently follows the message of Jesus and the Gospels, and these acts have attracted favourable comments and admiration.

Ecological education and spirituality

The final chapter of Francis's encyclical is entitled "Ecological Education and Spirituality". He implores us to limit our "compulsive consumerism" and "collective selfishness" (LS, 203-204). He charts a path by which individuals and nations can help the poor and rescue the planet. He urges environmental education which goes beyond providing information; he counsels us all to develop good habits and sound virtues for what he calls generous care for ecology and poor persons (LS, 203-210). This involves an "ecological conversion", which brings a change in lifestyle.

Support for Sustainable Development Goals

Francis reinforced his message on the plight of the environment and the poor when he visited President Obama, spoke to the US Congress, and then to the assembled delegates and heads of state at the United Nations. The message of the encyclical letter, however, is more specific when he discusses the costs of pollution, climate change and the plight of the poor, along with his proposed solutions. Francis urges personal actions and self-improvement but also advises us to go beyond that and engage our local communities and governments to develop policies and regulations that foster the spirit of generous care (LS, 219-221). His goals are thus much the same as those of the United Nations Sustainable Development Goals. But in addition, he asks us to develop what he calls "civic and political love" (LS, 228), recognizing that we need each other and have a shared responsibility for the planet and for the poor. In comparing Care for Our Common Home and the United Nations Sustainable Development Goals, an official of the World Bank said, "It is hard to imagine a more charismatic, disarming and inspirational champion for the very spirit of the sustainable development goals" (Taylor, 2015).

Criticisms of the encyclical

Most commentators on Pope Francis's Care for Our Common Home have been largely favourable (Hoffman, 2015b; Lowy, 2015; Reese, 2015; Sachs, 2015a, b).

They applaud his urgent concern for the global environment and poor peoples around the world. However, some critics find the encyclical to be lacking, and have spelled out their concerns. Let us examine some of these criticisms.

Understanding of capitalism is naive

The most common criticism of Francis's Care for Our Common Home is that he does not give sufficient credit to, appreciate, or perhaps even understand, the positive influence and results of free markets (Brooks, 2015; Montgomery, 2015; Will, 2015). These commentators acknowledge Francis's valuable emphasis on compassion, harmony and love as human motivations, and the benefits that result. But these same critics charge that he does not sufficiently recognize the positive effects of the "invisible hand", which sparks competition that in turn brings greater efficiencies and effectiveness in the free market. Some US critics say that he is narrowly influenced by his Latin American experiences and by European theologies. As a result, in their opinion he too negatively describes institutions in which people compete for economic gain and political power.

These critics go on to cite the benefits of free markets, noting how they produce needed goods and services and also provide jobs to hundreds of millions of people all over the world. Markets and technology have thus greatly reduced the number of people living in poverty globally and have increased life expectancy. This is especially apparent in China and India where hundreds of millions have been brought out of poverty. In addition, commentators point out that many nations are making progress recycling and reducing pollution. To achieve this they put to good use technology and markets (Brooks, 2015). Some critics have said that Francis overstates his case when he says that "The earth, our home, is beginning to look more and more like an immense pile of filth", because of our "throwaway culture" and industrial system (LS, 21-22).

A few commentators have been especially strong in their criticism. R. R. Reno, the editor of a conservative Catholic periodical, calls the encyclical "strikingly anti-scientific, anti-technological, and anti-progressive"; he compares it to Pius IX's 1864 Syllabus of Errors, with its "dismissal of the conceits of the modern era" (Reno, 2015). George Will is even stronger when he says that Francis's letter is "fact-free flamboyance", and ends his critique: "He stands against modernity, rationality, science and ultimately, the spontaneous creativity of open societies in which people and their desires are not problems but precious resources. Americans cannot simultaneously honor him and celebrate their nations' premises" (Will, 2015).

Carbon credits and water

Francis finds fault with "carbon credits" and "cap and trade" systems to reduce carbon pollution (LS, 171). But critics point out that these systems, using a market system, have worked in California and the north-east US. Some charge that

Francis idealizes the natural environment, yet "for most of mankind, nature has been, and remains scarcity, disease and natural disasters" (Will, 2015). David Brooks summarizes his more balanced critique,

> ... if we followed his line of reasoning ... There'd be no awareness that though industrialization can lead to catastrophic pollution in the short term (China), over the long haul both people and nature are better off with technological progress, growth and regulated affluence (Brooks, 2015).

Regarding water, Francis points out that it is scarce and precious in many parts of the world; and concerning it and all resources "wasting and discarding has reached unprecedented levels" (LS, 27). He seems inconsistent when he then goes on to say that access to safe drinking water is a human right (LS, 28-31). He does not acknowledge that putting some price on water is a method of reducing wasting water, rationing it and encouraging conservation.

Global regulation

Francis calls for additional global regulations (LS, 173-175). Indeed the 2015 Paris climate agreement of 195 nations requires that each nation present their plans for reducing carbon dioxide in the atmosphere. For generations the US has been the largest emitter of carbon, and has been criticized for being among the few developed nations that did not join earlier world agreements to reduce carbon. The US position has been that since developing nations, especially China and India, were not obliged to reduce their emissions, the US should not be required to do so. In spite of the US record, obtaining a global climate agreement in Paris was a priority for President Obama. Obama then worked to forge agreements prior to Paris with China and India, such that each nation would reduce its carbon emissions. Following the US signing of the global agreement, the US Environmental Protection Agency issued new regulations to reduce carbon from coal-fired power plants. This has met with opposition among coal companies, utilities, coal states and their legislators. Their opposition to new regulations is reinforced by the attitude that, for generations conservatives have feared that international regulations would lead to "world government" and a resulting "loss of US sovereignty".

On another issue, some critics say that Pope Francis does not acknowledge the positive influence that family planning and birth control can have in reducing poverty and decreasing the demand for resources, so he avoids the subject (Norris, 2013). Others point out that his letter is rooted in Christian Scripture and Catholic Social tradition, and thus is not relevant and does not speak to them. A brief summary of some of the contributions and criticisms of Francis's Care for Our Common Home is provided in Table 2.

Table 2 Care for Our Common Home: contributions and criticisms

Contributions	Criticisms
Deals with critical, urgent global issues: climate change and plight of poor people	Francis's understanding of free markets and capitalism is naïve and/or erroneous
Rooted in human dignity and the common good	Negative attitude towards competition within free markets
Underscores principal causes of the problems: individualism, selfishness, greed and the unregulated free market	Does not acknowledge that carbon "cap and trade" can be effective and has worked in some localities
Calls for a new mind-set, dialogue and "integral ecology", along with specific recommendations for persons and governments	Fails to sufficiently acknowledge reduction in global poverty through free markets
Challenges myths of unlimited resources, boundless growth and habits of "compulsive consumerism"	His call for global regulation could lead to loss of US sovereignty and world government
Broad consultation with scientists and other experts when preparing the letter	"... anti-scientific, anti-technological, and anti-progressive ..." (Reno, 2015) "... fact-free flamboyance ..." (Will, 2015)
Moral plea for action, based on Christian Scripture and Catholic social justice tradition	Based on Scripture and Catholic social tradition, so does not speak to all
Challenges all to shift to a simpler lifestyle and "less is more, so it is liberating"	Does not acknowledge tension between right to safe drinking water and water scarcity
Francis's personal humble lifestyle and helping poor people	Does not acknowledge world population growth and need for family planning
Francis has received much global attention and affirmation, and has an engaging and accessible writing style	President Obama's policy on coal and oil is an overreach of the agreement
Presented prior to Paris climate talks to support a successful agreement	However, critics acknowledge the importance of the issues

Reflections on Francis and his critics

Francis's comment that "Doomsday predictions can no longer be met with irony or disdain" (LS, 161) is sometimes criticized as overreach. Yet Francis is not alone, nor the first, to sound such a warning. More than a decade ago, in a prize-winning study, Jared Diamond of UCLA warned us about previous societies that did not attend to their natural environmental limits, which brought about their ruin (Diamond, 2005). Diamond examined dozens of historical civilizations from around the world that were prosperous, but the people failed to consider the limits imposed by their natural environment. In most cases, this led to decline and often to their catastrophic end. But Diamond was not the first to sound the alarm. We have received such warnings on the misuse of our planet's resources for decades (Meadows *et al.*, 1972; Schumacher, 1973). The fact that such careful, scientific, well-publicized work has had such little impact on US and global policy should ring alarm bells.

Common good

The principal quarrel with Francis centres on his emphasis on the common good of the entire community, including the planet. Rescuing the globe from environmental pollution, excess carbon emissions and climate change requires cooperation among all nations and peoples. Francis correctly maintains that the planet is "our common home", what philosophers call a "common good", and economists call a "commons" as in the "tragedy of the commons" (Hardin, 1968). In this same spirit, Francis's position is that the planet belongs to everyone, not just to those who own property, wealthy peoples or powerful nations. This modifies our views of the central importance of and privileges of private property and wealth, which often dominates our thinking and policies (Sayre, 2010). Thomas Donaldson of Wharton and James Walsh of the University of Michigan have set out a broader theory of business. They begin their incisive discussion with the probing dilemma: "Law is to justice, as medicine is to health, as business is to …" They ask how you would finish that sentence. Their answer in brief is that the role of the business system is to support the dignity of human beings (Donaldson and Walsh, 2015). Their theory closely aligns with the position of Francis.

Francis also calls on all people to be more conscious of "those on the margins", the poor, the disabled, the homeless, refugees, and those who most need our help. While acknowledging the importance of private property, he maintains that the right to private property is "not absolute" (LS, 93). Since writing the letter, Francis has also recognized that he often spoke of the few very wealthy and the vast majority of the global poor, but that he did not give sufficient attention to the growing hundreds of millions of people in the besieged middle class.

Predisposition and bias

When assessing problems, especially global issues, it is difficult for anyone to recognize their own biases. For those of us in the US, individualism and enlightened self-interest are foundational values. Yet often we are not aware that, among all nations, we are excessive on this score. When the attitudes of people in 53 nations of the world towards individualism and community were examined, the US ranked first in individualism and last in concern for the community (Hofstede, 2001). This helps to explain many of the strengths and weaknesses of the US character. Some of those weaknesses, such as selfishness and greed, now stand out (Hoffman, 2015a).

US individualism prolongs damage to our already fractured culture. This affects our business, political and community lives. Many people are unable or unwilling to understand or even listen to another's position, since they are convinced that their own opinion is correct. Their attitude is reinforced when they view media which supports, sometimes exclusively, their own views. Although the consequences of this attitude have become more pronounced in recent years, the basic attitude is not new. The limitations of US enlightened self-interest and individualism were summarized by Alexis de Tocqueville almost 200 years ago in his classic examination of American attitudes:

> ... Individualism proceeds from erroneous judgment more than depraved feelings; it originates as much in deficiencies of the mind as in perversity of heart ... individualism, at first, only saps the virtues of public life; but in the long run it attacks and destroys all others and is at length absorbed in downright selfishness (Tocqueville, 1946).

Tocqueville pinpointed probably the most serious weakness of the American character, and it is important to acknowledge such cultural blindness. Enlightened self-interest and individualism narrow one's perspective. Such an attitude encourages us to think less of public responsibilities, and it leads eventually to selfishness (Cavanagh, 2010).

Impact of the encyclical

Pope Francis's letter on climate change and its effect on the poor received some credit for the success of the Paris climate agreement. Moreover, it has influenced people globally, especially Catholic dioceses, parishes, schools and communities. The Philippines Catholic church has exercised leadership, as have religious communities in Australia. Catholic dioceses of Chicago, Atlanta, San Diego and San Francisco are urging energy efficiency and using solar sources for their buildings. The Catholic Climate Covenant has received a major boost, and the letter has led to plans for divestment from coal, oil and gas businesses among some Catholic institutions. Several African nations "have moved away from fossil fuels and forests as energy sources and adopt solar technology" (Roewe, 2016).

Carolyn Woo, President of Catholic Relief Services, and before that dean of Notre Dame University's Mendoza College of Business, directs her comments to business leaders:

> The message of this encyclical to the business world is a profoundly hopeful one, as it sees the potential of business as a force for good whose actions can serve to mitigate and stop the cumulative, compounding, irreversible, catastrophic effects of climate change driven by human actions (Woo, 2015).

In that spirit and as a result of Care for Our Common Home, *The Wall Street Journal* reported that in early 2016, "Global Business Leaders sought common ground with the Vatican on a range of ethical issues" at a joint two-day conference, in order to gain a better understanding and improve relations (Rocca, 2016).

Conclusions

Pope Francis, in Care for Our Common Home, raises urgent, fundamental and critical issues. Our common responsibilities for poor peoples, for reducing pollution and carbon in the atmosphere, and for addressing the excesses of unrestrained markets and technology are moral imperatives that cannot be ignored without lasting destructive consequences for us and for future generations. Yet when discussing these vital issues, we risk talking past one another. Francis urges us to listen to each other and to dialogue with a broader, humanistic, common good view of other peoples, our planet and our common goals.

Favourable reviews of Francis's letter have come from the scientific community as noted earlier. Leaders of many religious traditions have also applauded his position (Simons, 2012; Melino, 2015; Reuter, 2015; Waskow, 2015). Supporting his view, most religions oppose selfishness and "compulsive consumerism" and, more generally, urge a simpler lifestyle. In addition, the major conclusions of Francis's letter are based on the fundamental human virtues of prudence and wisdom. The most critical comments on the letter come from defenders of capitalism and free markets. Francis acknowledges the advantages of free markets, but he also outlines their moral limitations. When markets are detached from concern for others and the common good of the community and the planet, they become destructive. On a personal note, I have assigned and discussed this encyclical in class with graduate and undergraduate students of business, and the letter triggers new insights for them that are both enlightening and provocative. Many of the students then acknowledge their own wasteful and throw-away lifestyle and they conclude that they will adopt a simpler way of living.

Francis is becoming a worldwide prophet and ethical guide. He may now be the most respected and influential moral leader on the planet. *Fortune* magazine named him one of the top four of the "World's Greatest Leaders" for the last several years; in 2015 he was number one on the list (*Fortune*, 2016). Every person, nation and culture needs a prophet to prod them to reflect and to be true to their own goals and values. Pope Francis's principles, actions and words help to explain the worldwide influence he has had. There are few, if any, others on the world stage that provide such a vision and conscience for us all.

References

Brooks, D. (2015, June 23). Fracking and the Franciscans. *New York Times*, A23.

Cavanagh, G. (2010). *American Business Values: A Global Perspective* (6th ed.). Upper Saddle River, NJ: Prentice-Hall.

Damon, W. (1999). The moral development of children. *Scientific American*, 281, 72-78.

Dasgupta, P., & Ramanathan, V. (2015, September). Pursuit of the common good. *Science*, 19, 1457-1458.

Diamond, J. (2005). *Collapse: How Societies Choose to Fail or Succeed.* New York: Penguin Books.

Donaldson, T., & Walsh, J. (2015). Toward a theory of business. *Research in Organizational Behavior*, 35, 181-207.

Fortune (2016, April 1). Pope Francis: Head of the Roman Catholic Church. *Fortune*, 173(5), 81.

Francis I (2015). *Encyclical letter "Laudato Si": On Care for Our Common Home.* Vatican City: Vatican Press. Retrieved from: http://w2.vatican.va/content/francesco/en/encyclicals/documents/papa-francesco_20150524_enciclica-laudato-si.html

Hardin, G. (1968, December 13). The tragedy of the commons. *Science*.

Hoffman, A. (2015a). *How Culture Shapes the Climate Change Debate.* Palo Alto, CA: Stanford University Press.

Hoffman, A. (2015b). Laudato Si and the role of religion in shaping humanity's response to climate change. *Solutions*, 6(December), 40-47.

Hofstede, G. (2001). *Culture's Consequences.* Thousand Oaks, CA: Sage.

Incropera, F.P. (2015). *Climate Change, A Wicked Problem: Complexity and Uncertainty at the Intersection of Science, Economics, Politics, and Human Behavior.* New York: Cambridge University Press.

Kohlberg, L. (1978). The cognitive development approach to moral education. In P. Scharf (Ed.), *Readings in Moral Education* (pp. 36-51). Minneapolis: Winston Press.

Lowy, M. (2015, December). Laudato Si: The Pope's anti-systemic encyclical. *Monthly Review*, 67, 7.

Mahoney, D. (2015, October 10). Laudato Si and the Catholic social tradition. *National Review.*

McNutt, M. (2015). The Pope tackles sustainability. *Science*, 19(September), 1429.

Meadows, D.H., Meadows, D.L., Randers, J., & Behrens III, W.W. (1972). *Limits to Growth.* New York: Universe Books.

Melino, C. (2015, June 29). Dalai Lama endorses Pope Francis's encyclical on climate change. *EcoWatch.*

Montgomery, D. (2015, Fall). The flawed economics of Laudato Si. *The New Atlantis.*

Nature (2015, June 23). Editorial: Hope from the Pope. *Nature*, 522, 391.

Norris, F. (2013, September 21). Population growth forecast from the U.N. may be too high. *New York Times*, B3.

Reese, T. (2015, June 26). A reader's guide to Laudato Si. *National Catholic Reporter.*

Reno, R.R. (2015, June 18). The return of Catholic anti-modernism. *First Things.*

Reuter, T.A. (2015, October 16). The green revolution in the world's religions: Indonesian examples in international comparison. *Religions*, 6(4), 1217-1231.

Rieff, D. (2015). *The Reproach of Hunger: Food, Justice, and Money in the Twenty-first Century.* New York: Simon and Schuster.

Rocca, F.X. (2016, January 18). Business leaders move to strengthen Vatican ties. *Wall Street Journal.*

Roewe, B. (2016, June 16). Year-old Laudato Si has stirred up action for the earth. *National Catholic Reporter.*

Sachs, J.D. (2015a, May 18). A call to virtue. *America.*

Sachs, J.D. (2015b, July 6). The great gift of "Laudato Si". *America.*

Sayre, K.M. (2010). *Unearthed: The Economic Roots of Environmental Crisis*. South Bend, IN: University of Notre Dame Press.

Schumacher, E.F. (1973). *Small Is Beautiful: A Study of Economics As If People Mattered*. London: Blond & Briggs.

Simons, M. (2012, December 3). Orthodox leader deepens progressive stance on environment. *New York Times*.

Taylor, A.R. (2015, October 1). Caring for our common home: Pope Francis and the SDGs. *The World Bank*. Retrieved from: http://blogs.worldbank.org/climatechange/caring-our-common-home-pope-francis-and-sdgs-0

Tocqueville, A. (1946). *Democracy in America* (H. Reeve, Trans.), Vol. 2. New York: Knopf.

UN (2015). *Transforming Our World: The 2030 Agenda for Sustainable Development*. Retrieved from: https://sustainabledevelopment.un.org/post2015/transformingourworld

Wall Street Journal (2016, March 25). Pope Francis washes refugees' feet in holy week rite. *Wall Street Journal*, A1, A12.

Waskow, A. (2015, June 8). Pope Francis inspires 300+ rabbis to sign rabbinic letter on climate. *National Catholic Reporter*.

Will, G. (2015, September 18). Pope is a false prophet. *Washington Post*.

Woo, C. (2015). *Business insights from Laudato Si*. Retrieved from: http://en.radiovaticana.va/news/2015/06/18/business_insights_from_laudato_si/1152399

DOI: [10.9774/GLEAF.4700.2016.de.00009]

Corporate Social Responsibility in Light of Laudato Si*

Martijn Cremers

University of Notre Dame, USA

- Corporate social responsibility
- Catholic Social Teaching
- Laudato Si
- Social justice
- Solidarity
- Subsidiarity

This paper explores what Laudato Si teaches about corporate social responsibility. First, I highlight three key and interrelated themes in Laudato Si, namely that all of creation is a gift from a loving God, that "everything in the world is connected", and a call for a change in our personal response to God's gifts. Second, I relate these three themes to corporate social responsibility, considering the social purpose and nature of the corporation, the importance of cooperative relationships in solidarity for value creation in corporations, and our responsibility to others as a response to the gifts that we have received by practising subsidiarity. Third, I briefly discuss the practical implications using impact investing as an illustration.

K.J. Martijn Cremers joined the University of Notre Dame as Professor of Finance at the Mendoza College of Business in 2012. Prior to that, he was a faculty at Yale School of Management for ten years, from 2002 to 2012. He obtained his PhD in finance from the Stern School of Business at New York University in 2002. Hailing from the Netherlands, Professor Cremers' research focuses on empirical issues in investments and corporate governance. At Notre Dame, he teaches courses on investments, corporate governance and business ethics to MBA and undergraduate students.

264 Mendoza College of Business
University of Notre Dame
Notre Dame, IN 46556

mcremers@nd.edu

* I am grateful for the comments of colleagues and especially for those of Georges Enderle and Oliver Williams.

L AUDATO SI, THE RECENT ENCYCLICAL written by Pope Francis (2015), challenges us to reconsider our relationships with the environment, with each other, and ultimately with God. In this document, Pope Francis addresses "every person living on this planet" (LS, 3), calling for an inclusive dialogue. This paper explores what light this encyclical can shed on the concept of corporate social responsibility, and attempts to enter into a dialogue between corporate citizenship and this latest document of Catholic Social Teaching.

My focus will be on the view from Catholic Social Teaching (CST), a body of formal teachings of the Catholic Church of which Laudato Si is a part. In CST, our foremost responsibility is to act with justice, in the sense of giving others what they are due. Specifically, I primarily consider our corporate social responsibility towards giving others what they are due in *social* justice (which is sometimes also referred to as legal, general, common or contributive justice) in the corporate setting. Social justice pertains to what we owe to others in the community arising from their unconditional, fundamental dignity as human persons, irrespective of their particular or potential contributions to the community.[1] A major theme in Laudato Si is to expand social justice more explicitly to the whole natural environment of which we are a part. However, CST recognizes two other forms of justice as well, distributive and commutative, which are related to social justice and which Laudato Si also speaks to, but are left out of my discussion due to space constraints.[2]

I proceed in three parts. In the first part, I discuss three central themes that Pope Francis raises in Laudato Si, which are closely related.

The first theme is that all of creation is a *gift* from God arising from God's loving plan for His creation. These gifts include the gift of the natural environment, the gift of our very selves (who are creatures and thus part of nature but are also spiritual and thus able to transcend nature), and the gift of our relationships to all of creation, with other persons and especially with God the Creator. Laudato Si emphasizes the social or *shared purpose* of God's gifts, arguing that "the world is a gift which we have freely received and must share with others, [such that] ... solidarity is not optional but is rather a basic question of justice" (LS, 159).

The second theme is that "everything in the world is *connected*" (LS, 16). Pope Francis argues that "human life is grounded in three fundamental and closely intertwined relationships: with God, with our neighbor, and with the earth itself" (LS, 66), where the main problem is that each of "these three vital relationships have been broken" (LS, 66). Due to the intertwined nature of these relationships, Pope Francis argues that each of these three broken relationships

---

1 See the Catechism of the Catholic Church (CCC), 1928–1933.

2 Distributive justice pertains to what the community (especially those in positions of authority, wealth and power) owes all members of the community in proportion to their contribution and needs (CCC, 2411). Further, "[c]ontracts are subject to commutative justice, which regulates exchanges between persons and between institutions in accordance with a strict respect for their rights. Commutative justice obliges strictly; it requires safeguarding property rights, paying debts, and fulfilling obligations freely contracted. Without commutative justice, no other form of justice is possible" (CCC, 2411).

needs to be healed simultaneously, rejecting various reductionist solutions and instead explaining that "strategies for a solution [to our complex crisis] demand an integrated approach to combating poverty, restoring dignity to the excluded and at the same time protecting nature" (LS, 139).

The third theme in Laudato Si is such healing has to start with ourselves, i.e. with our *personal response*. In particular, Pope Francis writes that "it is we human beings above all who need to change" (LS, 202), arguing that "the ecological crisis is also a summons to profound interior conversion" (LS, 217). The encyclical explores in considerable detail what such change would look like in terms of the kinds of "new habits" or virtues of personal and social responsibility we need to develop.

In the second part, I explore what these three themes in Laudato Si—also in the context of Catholic Social Teaching (CST) more generally of which Laudato Si is a part (LS, 15)—teach about the purpose, priority and practice of the business corporation.

First, exactly because everything is a gift—and inherently social—CST argues that business corporations have a social purpose, such that those who control and own a corporation have a duty towards others and the natural environment. Such social responsibility means that "[b]usiness is a noble vocation, directed to producing wealth and improving our world" (LS, 129). This teaching that business corporations have a social purpose does not negate the right to private ownership of corporations, which is strongly defended in CST, but imposes limits on the just *use* of such ownership such that the benefits are shared rather than only accrue to those who own or control the corporation. As Pope Francis notes in Laudato Si, "God rejects every claim to absolute ownership" (LS, 67). Laudato Si warns against unjust situations where corporations impose negative externalities on the natural and social environment and care only about increasing productivity and profits but do not bring about "an integrally higher quality of life" (LS, 194) for everyone, especially those with least material wealth.

Second, because everything is connected, businesses can only achieve their social purpose through the just cooperation with all stakeholders, such that Laudato Si emphasizes the critical importance of "social capital: the network of relationships of trust, dependability, and respect for rules, all of which are indispensable for any form of civil coexistence" (LS, 128). I argue that corporations create value through the creation of "shared goods" with social, economic and environmental value, i.e. goods that can only be achieved through cooperation, including the products and services offered for sale, the human relationships among everyone involved, and the integral development of the persons working in the corporation. As a result, the priority of business is cooperation in *solidarity* as any value will only be created through connections: i.e. in cooperative relationships, where people recognize their mutual responsibilities and are willing to share their priorities in solidarity with others.

Third, the personal response required of each of us in turn requires that each person has the necessary freedom, opportunity, and help from others in order to develop one's ability to respond to each person's full potential. Accordingly, CST teaches that the practice of business should be characterized by *subsidiarity*, which is based on the centrality of genuine human freedom. Practising subsidiarity means that each person has room for personal initiative and creativity, and receives help from others to develop their particular skills and moral character, which comes with a corresponding duty to help others towards the same end. Subsidiarity supports cooperation in solidarity, allowing everyone to better contribute to the shared purpose of the corporation.

The third and final part concludes by summarizing what this understanding of the purpose, priority and practice of business implies for corporate social responsibility. Once again, the main implications are threefold.

First, we have a personal responsibility to respect others and our natural environment, i.e. our personal responsibility cannot be separated from our social responsibility. In other words, our duties towards others are not just up to us, because—in the understanding of Laudato Si—"everything is a gift, that we did not create ourselves nor nature, that we ourselves do not have the final word, that everything is not simply our property that we can use for ourselves alone or according to our wishes alone (LS, 6)". Corporate social responsibility thus entails a duty to ensure that the corporate strategy and the cooperation with all stakeholders contribute to human and environmental flourishing "in line with God's original gift of all that is" (LS, 5). As Laudato Si explains, this starts with respecting first and foremost the fundamental dignity of all human persons, and also, as the encyclical emphasizes, very much includes respecting the worth of all other creatures and all of creation as well.

Second, corporate social responsibility requires that a certain priority is given to "solidarity and a preferential option for the poorest of our brothers and sisters" (LS, 158), whom Laudato Si notes are particularly vulnerable to environmental, social, economic and political degradation. This is required in order to ensure justice, as those who

> ... have benefited from a high degree of industrialization ... have a greater responsibility for providing a solution to the problems they have caused (LS, 170)

and

> only when the economic and social costs of using up shared environmental resources are recognized with transparency and fully borne by those who incur them, not by other peoples or future generations can [business] actions be considered ethical (LS, 195).

Third, the most practical consequence for corporate social responsibility, beyond ensuring that any pollution or negative environmental impact is minimized, is to create a corporate environment that practices subsidiarity towards "integral human development and social inclusion" (LS, 109). This means that those in positions of authority, with superior power, information and control, have a responsibility to serve others, not just only "one's own immediate interests" (LS, 122). In particular, Pope Francis argues that "the current model, with its emphasis on success and self-reliance, does not appear to favor an investment in efforts to help the slow, the weak or the less talented to find opportunities in life" (LS, 196). Laudato Si challenges all of us to allow God and others to help us to change first and foremost ourselves and to grow in virtue both personally and socially in relationship with others. The encyclical calls us to "instill good habits" in ourselves and others, as "[o]nly by cultivating sound virtues will people be able to make a selfless ecological commitment" (LS, 211).

In my conclusion, I briefly discuss how "impact investing"—investing in businesses that create value through fulfilling neglected social or environmental needs, monitor the impact of everyone involved and operate in a competitive market environment—serves as a practical illustration of how corporate management and investors can implement these implications for corporate social responsibility.

Part 1: The three interrelated themes in Laudato Si

All is gift, arising from God's love

In Laudato Si, Pope Francis raises three central and interrelated themes. The first theme is essentially *theological*, namely that everything that exists is a gift from God, who created all out of love. As the document is addressed to "all people of good will" (LS, 62), the Pope's use of theological reflection is particularly challenging, as many to whom the letter is addressed may not be believers. He writes that "science and religion, with their distinctive approaches to understanding reality, can enter into an intense dialogue fruitful for both" (LS, 62), arguing that theological arguments have an important contribution to make:

> Given the complexity of the ecological crisis and its multiple causes, we need to realize that the solutions will not emerge from just one way of interpreting and transforming reality ... If we are truly concerned to develop an ecology capable of remedying the damage we have done, no branch of the sciences and no form of wisdom can be left out, and that includes religion and the language particular to it (LS, 63).

In the Judeo-Christian tradition, all of creation—including the natural environment and our own lives—is a wonderful *gift* from God arising from God's loving plan:

> Creation is of the order of love. God's love is the fundamental moving force in all created things: "For you love all things that exist, and detest none of the things that you have made; for you would not have made anything if you had hated it (*Wis* 11:24)" (LS, 77).

This idea is an appropriate starting point for understanding Laudato Si, as the natural first response to receiving wonderful gifts is to praise and thank the giver, which gives rise to the name of the encyclical (as Laudato Si means "Praise Be to You [my Lord]", referring to the hymn attributed to Saint Francis of Assisi, see LS, 87). The theological perspective that all of creation is a wonderful gift is also Pope Francis's starting point, influencing his subsequent approach to environmental and social problems and each person's responsibility towards solving these problems.

The idea that all of creation is a gift from God who loves us has the three following corollaries. First and foremost, it means that God has a "loving plan in which every creature has its own value and significance" (LS, 76), in which plan all gifts have a social or shared purpose, as "the world is a gift which we have freely received and must share with others, [such that] ... solidarity is not optional but is rather a basic question of justice" (LS, 159).

Second, the realization that God is the gift-giver and thus the Creator implies that we are creatures and ourselves part of the natural environment, and thus we need to recognize with humility our limits and our dependence on nature, on each other and on God. In particular, our happiness and flourishing are only realized within God's loving plan, neither independent of nor in opposition to it. Accordingly, Pope Francis warns against any "claim to absolute dominion", against "try[ing] to impose their own laws and interests on reality" (LS, 75).

Third, God's loving plan involves a particular role for human persons, who possess a "uniqueness which transcends the sphere of physics and biology" (LS, 81), as "each of us has his or her own personal identity and is capable of entering into dialogue with others and with God himself" (LS, 81), giving each human person a certain "pre-eminence" in creation, with a basic and fundamental dignity "which all human beings share in equal measure" (LS, 90). However, our unique role given to us by God is primarily that as stewards rather than owners (see LS, 67), where each person is given freedom that comes with a responsibility (i.e. a duty) of "caring, protecting, overseeing and preserving" (LS, 67).

All is connected

The second theme is that "everything in the world is *connected*" (LS, 16), which emphasizes co-dependence, relationality and co-responsibility. This means that we are not self-sufficient, but as creatures are dependent on nature, on each other and on God. Our connectedness is closely related to the first theme that everything is a gift from God arising from God's loving plan, as our connections are inherent in God's creation where "creatures exist only in dependence on each other, to complete each other, in the service of each other" (LS, 86).

Pope Francis identifies the main cause of our social and environmental problems as our lack of living according to this connectedness, arguing that "human life is grounded in three fundamental and closely intertwined relationships: with God, with our neighbor, and with the earth itself, [where each of] these three vital relationships have been broken, both outwardly and within us" (LS, 66), due to our presumption "to take the place of God and refusing to acknowledge our creaturely limitations", and the "false belief ... that there are no indisputable truths to guide our lives, and hence human freedom is limitless" (LS, 6). Quoting his predecessor, Pope Benedict XVI (2008), he argues that we need to "realize that creation is harmed where we ourselves have the final word, where everything is simply our property and we use it for ourselves alone. The misuse of creation begins when we no longer recognize any higher instance than ourselves, when we see nothing else but ourselves" (LS, 6).[3]

Due to their connectedness, Pope Francis argues that these three broken relationships need to be healed simultaneously, and thus he rejects reductionist solutions that focus on *only* technology, on *only* market-based solutions, or on *only* politics or regulation. This does not mean that he reject solutions that involve technology, markets or politics, but rather argues that none of these alone suffices and that each of these is connected, writing that "strategies for a solution [to our complex crisis] demand an integrated approach to combating poverty, restoring dignity to the excluded and at the same time protecting nature" (LS, 139). The necessity of such an integrated approach becomes clear once we realize "how inseparable the bond is between concern for nature, justice for the poor, commitment to society, and interior peace" (LS, 10).

A call for our personal response to change ourselves

The third theme is that the healing of our broken relationships with nature, with each other and with God has to start with ourselves, i.e. with our *personal response*, where Pope Francis argues that "it is we human beings above all who need to change" (LS, 202), arguing that "the ecological crisis is also a summons to profound interior conversion" (LS, 217). Such summons to change involves all of our relationships, i.e. to nature, to others and to God. As these are all inherently connected (the second theme), the pope concludes that "[t]here can be renewal of our relationship with nature without a renewal of humanity itself" (LS, 118).

The starting point of such renewal of all of our relationships is "an adequate anthropology" (LS, 118) that recognizes the special dignity of the human person, the importance of interpersonal relationships with others and God as well as our connections to the natural environment, and thus our responsibilities and duties towards others and nature. Importantly, the personal response that Pope Francis is advocating is not diminishing our dignity or freedom, but rather should help to heal our broken relationships with nature, each other and God, and should thus very much contribute to our overall flourishing and genuine freedom. As Pope Francis explains, "[h]uman beings cannot be expected to feel responsibility for the world unless, at the same time, their unique capacities of knowledge, will, freedom and responsibility are recognized and valued" (LS, 118).

Next, the renewal towards which Pope Francis invites us has both an individual-personal and a social aspect, both of which reflect our need for help (or to

---

3 This also echoes the conclusion of John Paul II (1995), who argued that:

> "[w]hen God is forgotten the creature itself grows unintelligible. Man is no longer able to see himself as mysteriously different from other earthly creatures; he regards himself merely as one more living being ... Enclosed in the narrow horizon of his physical nature, he is somehow reduced to being a thing, and no longer grasps the transcendent character of his existence as man. He no longer considers life as a splendid gift of God, something sacred entrusted to his responsibility and thus also to his loving care and veneration (Centesimus Annus, 22)."

receive gifts) and our call to use our gifts to help others, and thus directly relates to the first theme that all is gift. On the individual-personal level, Laudato Si call Christians to experience "an 'ecological conversion', whereby the effects of their encounter with Jesus Christ become evident in their relationship with the world around them" (LS, 217), namely "living our vocation to be protectors of God's handiwork (LS, 217)" as one example of living our social responsibility. On the social level, the encyclical argues that personal change alone is insufficient, especially because everything is connected, such that what is required is also a social change or "community conversion" (LS, 219), in order to facilitate a different social awareness that can only be achieved within a likeminded community.

In other words, the personal response that Laudato Si invites us towards is one that recognizes our social responsibility, and that in turn requires a social environment in which such recognition is widely shared. Pope Francis argues that it is difficult if not impossible to do this by ourselves, as "[i]solated individuals can lose their ability and freedom to escape the utilitarian mindset and end up prey to an unethical consumerism bereft of social or ecological awareness" (LS, 219). The encyclical explores in considerable detail what such change would look like in terms of the kind of "new habits" or virtues of personal responsibility we need to develop, starting with "an awareness of our common origin, of our mutual belonging, and of a future to be shared with everyone [enabling] ... the development of new convictions, attitudes and forms of life" (LS, 202). Therefore, this call for our personal response is also directly related to the second theme that all is connected.

Part 2: The social purpose, priority and practice of the business corporation

In this part, we consider how the three themes in Laudato Si can inform the social purpose, social priority and social practice of business corporations. The main development in Laudato Si, relative to the previous encyclicals, is to include greater concern for the natural environment, expanding but not contradicting the teachings in earlier encyclicals.

Social purpose

Business corporations have a *social purpose*, according to Catholic Social Teaching, exactly because everything is a gift with an inherently social nature and thus social purpose. Stating that business corporations have a social purpose does not negate the right to private ownership of corporations, which is strongly defended in CST, but rather argues for limits on the just *use* of such ownership. As Pope Francis writes in Laudato Si, "Christian tradition has never recognized the right to private property as absolute or inviolable, and has stressed the social purpose of all forms of private property" (LS, 93).

For example, John Paul II (1987) explained that

> [i]t is necessary to state once more the characteristic principle of Christian social doctrine: the goods of this world are originally meant for all. The right to private property is valid and necessary, but it does not nullify the value of this principle. Private property, in fact, is under a "social mortgage," which means that it has an intrinsically social function, based upon and justified precisely by the principle of the universal destination of material goods (Sollicitudo Rei Socialis, 42).

Pope Francis notes that

> [t]he principle of the subordination of private property to the universal destination of goods, and thus the right of everyone to their use, is a golden rule of social conduct and "the first principle of the whole ethical and social order" [involving] a social perspective which takes into account the fundamental rights of the poor and the underprivileged (LS, 93).[4]

The teaching that all is a gift with a social purpose, including business, naturally means that business has a social responsibility towards its social purpose. This challenges the view, famously articulated by Friedman (1970), that the *only* social responsibility of those who control corporations is to maximize the value for the investors, which Pope Francis calls a "misunderstanding of the very concept of the economy" (LS, 195), as this view seems based on an instrumental, reductionist and static approach to business: treating people and the environment as *only* means towards a financial end, reducing the attention to corporate impact to what can be measured in financial terms, and not accounting for the dynamic of wealth creation in a social organization within a diverse society with great inequalities.[5]

To start with the latter, the recognition of a social purpose is particularly important in situations where corporations can impose negative externalities on the natural and social environment, which may increase productivity and profits but do not bring about "an integrally higher quality of life" (LS, 194) for

---

4 John Paul II (1991) explains the meaning of the social purpose of corporations in more detail, writing that

> "ownership ... is [only] just and legitimate if it serves useful work, [which is work that] ... (i) provides for the needs of his family, his community, his nation, and ultimately all humanity, (ii) ... collaborates in the work of his fellow employees, as well as in the work of suppliers and in the customers' use of goods, in a progressively expanding chain of solidarity, (iii) ... where man fulfils himself by using his intelligence and freedom (43)."

On the other hand, he warns that

> "it becomes illegitimate, however, when it is not utilized [towards useful work] or when it serve to impede the work of others, in an effort to gain a profit which is not the result of the overall expansion of work and the wealth of society, but rather is the results of curbing them or of illicit exploitation, speculation or the breaking of solidarity among working people. Ownership of this kind has no justification, and represents an abuse in the sight of God and man (Centesimus Annus, 43)."

5 For a recent, extensive discussion on the various views on corporate social responsibility, see Williams (2014).

everyone, especially those with least material wealth and opportunity. Arguing that there are many examples of negative externalities that are not reflected in market prices, Pope Francis writes that

> ... it should always be kept in mind that environmental protection cannot be assured solely on the basis of financial calculations of costs and benefits. The environment is one of those goods that cannot be adequately safeguarded or promoted by market forces.[6] Once more, we need to reject a magical conception of the market, which would suggest that problems can be solved simply by an increase in the profits of companies or individuals. Is it realistic to hope that those who are obsessed with maximizing profits will stop to reflect on the environmental damage which they will leave behind for future generations? Where profits alone count, there can be no thinking about ... the complexity of ecosystems which may be gravely upset by human intervention, [and] ... biodiversity is considered at most a deposit of economic resources available for exploitation, with no serious thought for the real value of things, their significance for persons and cultures, or the concerns and needs of the poor (LS, 190).

Therefore, Laudato Si also challenges the view that maximizing shareholder wealth is generally the best approach to ensure benefits to all stakeholders, as often argued by finance and management scholars (Sundaram and Inkpen, 2004).

More generally, CST views the corporation as a social organization in which we can responsibly use and develop our gifts in freedom, in relationship with others, and contribute to others in a way that we couldn't individually—i.e. the corporation is a community of persons who get together for the sake of satisfying both individual and social purposes (Melé, 2011). The understanding of the corporation as a community of persons that has a shared purpose (i.e. a "common good") contrasts with both of the most prevalent views of the corporation, namely shareholder wealth maximization and stakeholder theory (see, e.g. Abela, 2001; Cortright and Naughton, 2002; Garvey, 2003; Cremers, 2016). On the one hand, the typical finance view sees the corporation as a "nexus of contracting" that is owned by shareholders (Jensen and Meckling, 1978), with the primary or sole responsibility to maximize shareholder value (Sundaram and Inkpen, 2004) and denying the existence of social responsibility that is unrelated to shareholder value (Friedman, 1970), even if a focus on shareholder value implies an instrumental (but *only* instrumental) interest in stakeholder welfare (Dobson, 1999). On the other hand, stakeholder theory tends to focus on the legitimate and intrinsic interests of each of the different stakeholders (Donaldson and Preston, 1995), rather than on their shared, social purpose that brings them together in order to create "shared value" (Porter and Kramer, 2011).

However, the idea that a corporation has a social purpose—and thus that those in positions of authority at corporations have a corresponding social responsibility—does not mean that corporations should not give shareholders a just return on their investment as a compensation for their risk-taking,

---

6 Quoting the Pontifical Council for Justice and Peace's (2005) "Compendium of the Social Doctrine of the Church".

let alone that profits do not matter, as firms that lose too much money will go bankrupt. Rather, Abela (2001, p. 111) explains that, in e.g. John Paul II (1991), Catholic Social Teaching "endorses the importance of profit as one aspect of the purpose of business" (Centesimus Annus, 34-35). However, this endorsement is clearly qualified, so that profit is not the most important aspect of the firm's purpose; in fact at most it is only equal to the other aspects of the purpose of the firm. John Paul II (1991) states that "other human and moral factors must also be considered [besides profit] which, in the long term, are at least equally important for the life of a business" (Centesimus Annus, 35).

The social purpose of corporations can also be understood economically. Corporations create value through the creation of "shared goods" with social, economic and environmental value, where shared goods are goods that can only be achieved through cooperation in a social organization such as a corporation. These shared goods include the products and services offered for sale, the human relationships among everyone involved with the corporation, and the integral development of the persons working in the corporation. This means that the process of value creation in corporations—through hierarchical coordination towards socially beneficial cooperation (Rajan and Zingales, 1998)—is different from the process of value creation in markets. Markets create value through a process of competitive bargaining about individual transactions, giving rise to not just individual but also social (potential) benefits, such as allowing information to be shared across the market, risk-sharing or co-insurance among all market participants and creating more opportunities to participate and better allocation of resources and capital. While markets require institutions and regulations, the market mechanism can create these social benefits even if market participants, institutions and regulations are only concerned with—and are responsible for—the particular transaction. The distinctive process of value creation in corporations versus markets means that corporations can both benefit from the disciplinary pressure of operating in a market environment and suffer from a "race to the bottom" in the face of short-term market pressure (Phelps, 2010).

Shared goods are thus created primarily through cooperation rather than competition. Cooperation takes place within social connections, i.e. in cooperative relationships. Therefore, in order to achieve their social purpose, the important social priority in firms is having just relationships of *solidarity* with all of the corporate stakeholders, i.e. generating "social capital: the network of relationships of trust, dependability, and respect for rules, all of which are indispensable for any form of civil coexistence" (LS, 128). The centrality of social capital brings in the second theme of the encyclical, of connectedness, and is more broadly discussed by Benedict XVI (2009), who writes that

> traditional principles of social ethics like transparency, honesty and responsibility cannot be ignored or attenuated ... [I]n commercial relationships the principle of gratuitousness and the logic of gift as an expression of fraternity can and must find their place within normal economic activity. This is a human demand at the present time, but it is also demanded by economic logic. It is a demand both of charity and of truth (Caritas in Veritate, 36).

The Church's social doctrine has always maintained that justice must be applied to every phase of economic activity, because this is always concerned with man and his needs. Locating resources, financing, production, consumption and all the other phases in the economic cycle inevitably have moral implications. Thus every economic decision has a moral consequence (CiV, 37).

[E]conomic life must be understood as a multi-layered phenomenon: in every one of these layers, to varying degrees and in ways specifically suited to each, the aspect of fraternal reciprocity must be present. In the global era, economic activity cannot rescind from gratuitousness, which fosters and disseminates solidarity and responsibility for justice and the common good among the different economic players. It is clearly a specific and profound form of economic democracy. Solidarity is first and foremost a sense of responsibility on the part of everyone with regard to everyone, and it cannot therefore be merely delegated to the State (CiV, 38).

Building on this earlier teaching, Pope Francis also argues that solidarity is both a moral and an economic imperative, as "human costs always include economic costs, and economic dysfunctions always involve human costs" (LS, 128). At the same time, however, Pope Francis warns repeatedly against a purely instrumental approach, warning against "the technocratic paradigm" in which one "accepts every advance in technology with a view to profit, without concern for its potentially negative impact on human beings" (LS, 109). As an example that solidarity is first a moral demand, Laudato Si argues that "only when the economic and social costs of using up shared environmental resources are recognized with transparency and fully borne by those who incur them, not by other peoples or future generations can [business] actions be considered ethical" (LS, 195).

In an instrumental approach, where solidarity is only practised to the extent that it does not adversely affect financial wealth, "economic interests easily end up trumping the common good and manipulating information so that their own plans will not be affected" (LS, 54). In the end, Pope Francis warns us that there are no "purely" instrumental approaches, as there is a moral consequence to every market-based or technological decision:

We have to accept that technological products are not neutral, for they create a framework which ends up conditioning lifestyles and shaping social possibilities along the lines dictated by the interests of certain powerful groups. Decisions which may seem purely instrumental are in reality decisions about the kind of society we want to build (LS, 107).

Solidarity involves sharing in both the fruits and the risks of the corporation, and it entails avoiding situations where some stakeholders benefit at the cost of other stakeholders or to the exclusion of other stakeholders. More generally, solidarity implies that people recognize their social responsibilities, i.e. their mutual and reciprocal duties, and are willing to actually share priorities, and thus serve each other. This in turn means that all stakeholders—and especially those with superior information, power and control in the corporation—need to have a long-term *commitment* towards the social purpose of the firm and the good of the other stakeholders (Mayer, 2013). This is both a moral and an economic issue (see Cremers and Sepe, 2016).

Finally, in order to achieve the particular social purpose of a corporation, and arising within cooperative relationships of solidarity that constitute the corporation's social priority, each person needs in practice to contribute in their specific capacity and to their best individual ability to the shared goods. This requires that each person involved in the corporation can participate in genuine freedom, has opportunity to learn and grow, and receives help towards developing their abilities. Pope Francis underlines in Laudato Si that work "should be the setting for this rich personal growth, where many aspects of life enter into play: creativity, planning for the future, developing our talents, living out our values, relating to others, giving glory to God" (LS, 127). As he writes, "[w]e were created with a vocation to work, [which] … is a necessity, part of the meaning of life on this earth, a path to growth, human development and personal fulfilment" (LS, 128). This is consonant with the third theme in Laudato Si that calls for our personal change towards social responsibility, which asserts that change should be made in genuine freedom in order to be consistent with our dignity (i.e. genuine freedom for all stakeholders, see further Laudato Si, 182-183, which emphasizes free exchange of views, transparency, lack of economic or political pressure, consensus building, etc.).

Given the fundamental importance of freedom, opportunity and receiving help for personal growth and fulfilment, CST proposes subsidiarity as the basic social practice in business. Subsidiarity, based on the centrality of human freedom, was defined by Pope Pius XI (1931) in Quadragesimo Anno as the principle that

> [j]ust as it is gravely wrong to take from individuals what they can accomplish by their own initiative and industry and give it to the community, so also it is an injustice and at the same time a grave evil and disturbance of right order to assign to a greater and higher association what lesser and subordinate organizations can do. For every social activity ought of its very nature to furnish help to the members of the body social, and never destroy and absorb them (Quadragesimo Anno, 79).

As result, practising subsidiarity means that each person has room for personal initiative and creativity, and receives help from others in developing their particular skills and moral character, and that particular care is taken to avoid harm (including, as Laudato Si emphasizes, environmental harm) to the stakeholders with least economic power. Inherently related to solidarity, subsidiarity implies that all interested stakeholders have not only a "negative" freedom not to be harmed, but also have a right to genuine "positive" freedom to participate and to receive help (at the appropriate levels), which comes with a reciprocal duty to give others that freedom and help. Subsidiarity is also dependent on what Laudato Si calls, for example, "personal qualities of self-control and willingness to learn from one another" (LS, 214) and "a spirit of generous care" (LS, 220). The encyclical argues that these are threatened by "the 'myths' of a modernity grounded in a utilitarian mindset (individualism, unlimited progress, competition, consumerism, the unregulated market)" (see LS, 210), which is a disposition that requires a personal and social conversion to be overcome.

Part 3: Implications for corporate social responsibility

This part concludes, with a summary of what this understanding from CST of the social purpose, the social priority and the social practice of business implies for corporate social responsibility. Once again, the main implications are threefold.

The first implication is that our personal responsibility includes a social responsibility, that we have a duty towards others that is not just up to us, which includes a duty to respect others and our natural environment. Therefore, corporate social responsibility entails a duty to ensure that the corporate strategy and the cooperation with all stakeholders contribute to human and environmental flourishing "in line with God's original gift of all that is" (LS, 5). As the encyclical explains, the starting point is the recognition of the fundamental dignity of all human persons, which Laudato Si argues cannot be separated from respecting the worth of all other creatures and all of creation as well.

Laudato Si argues that "our irresponsible behavior" has damaged both the natural and social environments, which Pope Francis argues are both

> ... ultimately due to the same evil: the notion that there are no indisputable truths to guide our lives, and hence human freedom is limitless. We have forgotten that "man is not only a freedom which he creates for himself. Man does not create himself. He is spirit and will, but also nature".

In effect, Laudato Si forcefully rejects a relativistic stance and argues that the starting point for corporate social responsibility is to recognize that everything is a gift with an inherently social dimension, that we did not create ourselves nor nature, that we ourselves do not have the final word, that everything is not simply our property that we can use for ourselves alone or according to our wishes alone (LS, 6): we have a social responsibility or duties towards others, whether or not we are willing or able to recognize it. "Man must respect the particular goodness of every creature, to avoid any disordered us of things" (LS, 69).

The second implication for corporate social responsibility is that, while "everything is connected" and all stakeholders should benefit from the involvement in the corporation, a real priority should be given to "solidarity and a preferential option for the poorest of our brothers and sisters" (LS, 158), whom Laudato Si notes are particularly vulnerable to environmental, social, economic and political degradation. Given the vast inequalities among persons, Pope Francis argues that what is necessary is "before all else an appreciation of the immense dignity of the poor in the light of our deepest convictions as believers". Therefore, solidarity with those who are most vulnerable is required in justice because of their fundamental dignity, while those who "have benefited from a high degree of industrialization ... have a greater responsibility for providing a solution to the problems they have caused" (LS, 170).

The third and most practical implication for corporate social responsibility, beyond ensuring that any pollution or negative environmental impact is minimized, is to create a corporate environment that practises subsidiarity towards "integral human development and social inclusion" (LS, 109). This is based on the fundamental importance of genuine human freedom, including in the economic realm. Subsidiarity means that those in positions of authority, with superior power, information and control, have a responsibility to serve others, not only "one's own immediate interests" (LS, 122). In particular, Pope Francis argues that "the current model, with its emphasis on [individualist] success and self-reliance, does not appear to favor an investment in efforts to help the slow, the weak or the less talented to find opportunities in life" (LS, 196).

Practising subsidiarity also implies an openness to receive and learn oneself. In particular, Laudato Si challenges all of us to allow God and others to help us to change first and foremost ourselves, to grow in virtue both personally and socially in relationships with others. The encyclical thus calls us to "instill good habits" (LS, 211) in ourselves and others, as "[o]nly by cultivating sound virtues will people be able to make a selfless ecological commitment" (LS, 211).

Conclusion

Three central themes in Laudato Si—all of creation is a gift from a loving God with a social purpose, that "everything in the world is connected", and a call for our personal response to God's connected gifts, i.e. a conversion—suggest a particular view of corporate social responsibility. In particular, Pope Francis concludes in Laudato Si that corporate social responsibility is not optional but a moral duty. This implies that corporations have a social purpose, or "common good", to contribute to human flourishing in a thriving natural environment. As a result, corporate social responsibility entails a duty towards ensuring that the strategy, human talent and corporate resources contribute to the social purpose of the corporation, in such a way that all stakeholders benefit in cooperative relationships of solidarity and subsidiarity.

A specific way in which this can be implemented is "impact investing"— investing in businesses that create value through fulfilling neglected social or environmental needs, monitor the impact of everyone involved and operate in a competitive market environment, see e.g. Bugg-Levine and Emerson (2011) and Rodin and Brandenburg (2014).[7] In my view, "impact investments" have three key characteristics. First, their corporate strategy directly links social and environmental needs to the creation of financial wealth, such that achieving positive social or environmental impact is an inherent part of the corporate strategy that drives financial success. Therefore, the corporate strategy is explicitly focused on contributing to the firm's social purpose. Second, these businesses collect and monitor data on how all stakeholders are impacted, including investors, employees, customers and the natural environment. This data is used to hold

---

7 Further, impact investing seems broadly consistent with the Principles for Responsible Investment (PRI, see http://www.unpri.org) and the sustainable development goals adopted by the United Nations in 2015 (see http://www.unglobalcompact.org/what-is-gc/our-work/sustainable-development).

internal managers accountable and to increase transparency towards external investors. While such data will always be inherently incomplete and its use does not guarantee solidarity, my hope is that increased transparency and accountability regarding social and environmental impact facilitate solidarity. Third, these firms operate in a competitive market environment, which may increase discipline and efficiency and thereby facilitate economic sustainability as well.

Laudato Si effectively invites all corporate executives to ensure that social and environmental impact assessment "should not come after the drawing up of a business proposition", but rather "be part of the process from the beginning" (LS, 183), and in my view invites all investors to behave like impact investors.

References

Abela, A.V. (2001). Profit and more: Catholic social teaching and the purpose of the firm. *Journal of Business Ethics*, 31, 107-116.

Benedict XVI (2008, January 8). *Address to the Diplomatic Corps Accredited to the Holy See*. Retrieved from: http://w2.vatican.va/content/benedict-xvi/en/speeches/2007/january/documents/hf_ben-xvi_spe_20070108_diplomatic-corps.html

Benedict XVI (2009). *Encyclical letter "Caritas in Veritate"*. Vatican City: Vatican Press. Retrieved from: http://w2.vatican.va/content/benedict-xvi/en/encyclicals/documents/hf_ben-xvi_enc_20090629_caritas-in-veritate.html

Bugg-Levine, A., & Emerson, J. (2011). *Impact Investing: Transforming How We Make Money While Making a Difference*. San Francisco: Jossey-Bass.

Cortright, S.A., & Naughton, M.J. (Eds.). (2002). *Rethinking the Purpose of Business: Interdisciplinary Essays from the Catholic Social Tradition*. Notre Dame, IN: University of Notre Dame Press.

Cremers, M. (2016). What corporate governance can learn from Catholic social teaching. *Journal of Business Ethics*, forthcoming.

Cremers, M., & Sepe, S. (2016). The shareholder value of empowered boards. *Stanford Law Review*, 68(1), 67-148.

Dobson, J. (1999). Is shareholder wealth maximization immoral? *Financial Analyst Journal*, 55(5), 69-75.

Donaldson, T., & Preston, L.E. (1995). The stakeholder theory of the corporation: Concepts, evidence, and implications. *Academy of Management Review*, 20(1), 65-91.

Francis I (2015). *Encyclical letter "Laudato Si": On Care for Our Common Home*. Vatican City: Vatican Press. Retrieved from: http://w2.vatican.va/content/francesco/en/encyclicals/documents/papa-francesco_20150524_enciclica-laudato-si.html

Friedman, M. (1970, September 13). The social responsibility of business is to increase its profits. *New York Times Magazine*.

Garvey, G.E. (2003). The theory of the firm, managerial responsibility, and Catholic social teaching. *Journal of Markets and Morality*, 6(2), 525-540.

Jensen, M., & Meckling, W. (1976). Theory of the firm: Managerial behavior, agency costs and capital structure. *Journal of Financial Economics*, 3, 305-360.

John Paul II (1987). *Encyclical letter "Sollicitudo Rei Socialis"*. Vatican City: Vatican Press.

John Paul II (1991). *Encyclical letter "Centesimus Annus"*. Vatican City: Vatican Press.

John Paul II (1995). *Encyclical letter "Evangelium Vitae"*. Vatican City: Vatican Press.

Mayer, C. (2014). *Firm Commitment: Why the Corporation is Failing Us and How to Restore Trust in it*. Oxford: Oxford University Press.

Melé, D. (2011). The firm as a "community of persons": A pillar of humanistic business ethos. *Journal of Business Ethics*, 106(1), 89-101.

Phelps, E.S. (2010). Short-termism is undermining America. *New Perspectives Quarterly*, 27, 17-19.

Pius XI (1931). *Encyclical letter "Quadragesimo Anno"*. Vatican City: Vatican Press.

Pontifical Council for Justice and Peace (2005). *Compendium of the Social Doctrine of the Church*. Washington, DC: United States Conference of Catholic Bishops.

Porter, M.E., & Kramer, M.R. (2011). Creating shared value—how to reinvent capitalism—and unleash a wave of innovation and growth. *Harvard Business Review*, January-February, 1-17.

Rajan, R., & Zingales, L. (1998). Power in a theory of the firm. *Quarterly Journal of Economics*, May, 387-432.

Rodin, J., & Brandenburg, M. (2014). *The Power of Impact Investing: Putting Markets to Work for Profit and Global Good*. Philadelphia: Wharton Digital Press.

Sundaram, A.K., & Inkpen, A.C. (2004). The corporate objective revisited. *Organization Science*, 15(3), 350-363.

Williams, O.F. (2014). *Corporate Social Responsibility: The Role of Business in Sustainable Development*. Abingdon, UK and New York: Routledge.

DOI: [10.9774/GLEAF.4700.2016.de.00010]

How Pope Francis is Shaping the Environment of Business

Mark R. Kennedy

University of North Dakota, USA

Ricardo Calleja

IESE Business School (University of Navarra), Spain

It is vital for businesses to understand the flows of social trends and the need to actively engage with shapeholders—political, regulatory, media and activist actors that may not care about an organization's success, but have a significant ability to shape an organization's risks and opportunities. Pope Francis—besides the moral authority of his office—has shown an outstanding ability to navigate a challenging social context advancing his agenda, and to place himself as a shapeholder for governments, international organizations and businesses—particularly after the publication of his much praised Encyclical "Laudato Si" on the ecology and integral human development. In this paper we explore both aspects of Francis's political record, to draw lessons for business's exercise of corporate citizenship in engaging with their social and political landscape, and to map some of the trends shaped by Francis, that business leaders will need to engage in the foreseeable future. We consider the currents that are disrupting economic and power structures using Francis's teachings in Laudato Si. We discuss the genius of Pope Francis's civic engagement in turning risks into opportunities, highlighting lessons in exercising global citizenship for businesses operating in global markets. For this purpose, we will make use of Francis's official documents and public interventions, some background literature to put his teachings in context, as well as media reactions and the incipient scholarly commentaries on his trajectory.

- Corporate citizenship
- Shapeholders
- Pope Francis
- Ecology
- Sustainability

Mark Kennedy is currently President of the University of North Dakota (UND). Kennedy brings an unmatched range of global experiences as a senior executive at one of America's largest companies (Macy's), serving as a US Congressman, advising both Presidents George W. Bush and Barack Obama on international trade, and leading George Washington University's (GWU) Graduate School of Political Management (GSPM). In his forthcoming book from Columbia Business School Press on *Engaging to Win*, Kennedy updates the rules for business engagement with society reflecting the rise of activism and expanded political involvement in commercial affairs. He reveals how understanding the views of others and converting sceptics to embrace your aims are the keys to success, whether you are collaborating or competing. Kennedy introduced the concept of "Shapeholders" to the field of business strategy—the political, regulatory, media and activist actors that shape a firm's opportunities and risks. Kennedy reveals how to effectively engage shapeholders both at home and abroad to profitably advance business strategies while benefiting society. Kennedy is Chairman of the Economic Club of Minnesota and a member of the Council on Foreign Relations. A graduate of St John's University, Kennedy received a Master's in Business Administration (MBA) with distinction from the University of Michigan.

mark@markkennedy.com

Ricardo Calleja is a Senior Lecturer in Business Ethics at IESE Business School (University of Navarra, Spain). He holds a PhD in Legal and Political Philosophy from Universidad Complutense de Madrid and has been a visiting scholar at Catholic University of America and Mendoza College of Business (University of Notre Dame, Indiana), and lectured at several universities in Spain, Latin America and the US. His research is focused on the implications of the Aristotelian-Thomist tradition for business management and governance, and on ethical questions regarding business–government relationship. He was the director of a residence hall at Universidad Complutense and is involved in a number of educational and civil society initiatives in his home country.

ricardocalleja@gmail.com

THE 2016 OSCAR AWARDS CEREMONY, among the most secular of events, concluded with awardees nodding to Pope Francis, confirming the impact of his surprising papacy. Best Actor awardee Leonardo DiCaprio appealed for action on climate change, expressing concern for the "billions and billions of underprivileged people who would be the most affected by this",[1] framing the issue in the manner Francis introduced. In doing so, Francis changed the narrative, facilitating a successful climate summit in Paris. Michael Sugar, the producer of the Best Movie, *Spotlight*, concluded his remarks by saying, "Pope Francis, it's time to protect the children and restore the faith".[2] Sugar's appeal to the pontiff reflected a view that Francis was responsive to societal concerns and changing the course of events.

When even the most earthly of institutions calls for action to "restore the faith", it is clear that Pope Francis has been effective at engaging society and steering the Church on a path that leads even those who are not its adherents to consider it a force for good.

The failure to imitate Francis's effective engagement permits businesses to be portrayed as a force for ill. It is not enough for businesses to incorporate social concerns about their individual operations into their strategic direction, including those Francis highlights in his Encyclical "Laudato Si" on the ecology and integral human development (the title evoking a poem by Saint Francis of Assisi, the most popular of Catholic saints) (Kell *et al.*, 2015). They must also follow Francis's example of strategically engaging social actors so that the public believes their company and free enterprise delivers benefits for the many, not just the few.

Effective social relations requires more than constructive relations with those that have a stake in your success, like your customers, employees, suppliers and local communities. It also demands astutely engaging **shapeholders**—political, regulatory, media and social activist actors that may not care about an organization's success, but have a significant ability to shape an organization's risks and opportunities (Kennedy, 2013).

Pope Francis—besides the moral authority of his office—has shown an outstanding ability to navigate challenging shapeholder relations to advance his agenda. In so doing he became a *shapeholder* himself for governments, international organizations and businesses—particularly after the publication of the Encyclical Laudato Si on the ecology and integral human development.

In electing Francis as Pope, the experienced and global-minded club of Cardinals chose an outsider, a Latin American, someone able to take the wheel in his own hands. All popes have the capacity to deeply influence the direction of history due to the prestige of the office and the persons holding it. In his first three years of service, Pope Francis has gone beyond the expectation of his electors revealing a capacity—and a willingness—to shape central aspects of contemporary culture, politics and economics. That has captured the attention of public opinion (Allen, 2014).

---

1 Retrieved from: https://www.youtube.com/watch?v=AO0P56eXtzM
2 Retrieved from: https://www.youtube.com/watch?v=3XyfZ79mpX0

In this paper we explore how Francis's political record provides lessons for business's exercise of corporate citizenship in engaging with their social and political landscape. We will discuss the genius of Pope Francis's civic engagement in turning risks into opportunities. We also explore Francis's teachings and emphasis in his aforementioned Encyclical, pointing to future challenges for business. Pope Francis has been engaging them in a way that strengthened the Church while upping the pressure even more for flat-footed enterprises. Let's focus first on how Pope Francis has engaged with these challenges and created new opportunities, within the Church and in the global arena.

We contrast how corporate actors in exercising their global citizenship have not been nearly as effective in advocating for the free enterprise system upon which they depend as Francis has for the poor and the environment. We will consider some lessons that business leaders could learn and apply in the exercise of a proactive corporate citizenship that is eager to engage with challenges, instead of just reacting to crisis. In the words of Aßländer and Curbach (2014), to turn from *bourgeois* into *citoyens* (in the sense of actively participative citizens).

For this purpose, we will make extensive use of Francis's official documents and public interventions, some background literature to put his teachings in context, as well as media reactions and the incipient scholarly commentaries on his trajectory.

Seven steps for shapeholder success

For business leadership to exercise political wisdom—as a part of the virtue of practical wisdom (*phrónesis* or *prudentia*)—demands circumspection and providence: the ability to grasp the reality of the environment and the trends that are shaping the future (Calleja and Melé, 2016). Only then are businesses capable of advancing the long-term best interests of their company by contributing to the common good of society at large. A key part of that surrounding reality is constituted by a certain type of actor—shapeholders.

According to Mark Kennedy's definition (2013), shapeholders are political, regulatory, media and activist actors lacking a significant natural stake in their success, but whose actions can shape, constrain or expand a firm's opportunities or risks. It is important for businesses to appreciate the need to treat those societal actors that have little or no stake in their success differently from true stakeholders like their employees, suppliers and customers.

Effective shapeholder engagement can boost a company's sales, as Toyota realized when California allowed its Prius and other hybrid vehicles to use high occupancy vehicle lanes with a single passenger (Voelcker, 2010). As Uber found out, shapeholders also have the ability to limit the success of any organization, particularly those that seek to overturn entrenched industry structures (Reuters, 2016).

Mark Kennedy's approach to effective shapeholder engagement takes a long-term view of the most beneficial path for organizations to engage with shapeholders. It identifies Seven Steps to Shapeholder Success—two sets of As. The first set of As—Align, Anticipate and Assess—define how to be well positioned with respect to shapeholder actions (Kennedy, 2016). The second set of As—Avert, Acquiesce; Advance and Assemble—explain how to act in response to an attack or opportunity posed by shapeholders.

This approach is complementary with other corporate citizenship accounts such as that advanced by Simon Zadek that explain how corporations become good corporate citizens through different phases of a learning process: defensive, compliant, managerial, strategic and civil (Zadek, 2004). A full implementation of the shapeholder approach demands reaching the *civil* step. According to Alejo José G. Sison (2009), for cultural reasons reflecting an underlying philosophy, American firms might find it more difficult than their European counterparts to adapt their culture to this approach.

Pope Francis's success in altering the perception of the Church he leads and in setting the terms of debate reflects his practice of the Seven Steps to Shapeholder Success. Francis plays his role so effectively that he shapes the socioeconomic currents that business people will have to navigate to be able to effectively operate in society.

In implementing these seven steps, it is important that business leaders understand Francis's attitudes, method of engaging challenges and how he pushes his agenda. They must appreciate how Francis's words, deeds, symbolic gestures and rhetorical emphasis shape the deep currents that are likely to contour our public conversation in the years to come. In this regard, Francis is not infallible, but has become one of the most important compasses for global leaders. This proposition holds whether we agree with his views or not.

Throughout our discussion, we draw insights mainly from Laudato Si (LS hereafter), Francis's Encyclical on ecology, but we recommend paying attention to other texts as well, in particular his discourses to prominent political assemblies and civic groups (the UN General Assembly, the US Congress, the European Parliament, Discourse to the Bolivian movements, etc.). [3] By intelligently addressing the demands and suggestions from the Pontiff, business can be certain that they would be raising their sails to a lasting wind.

Francis as shapeholder

Before taking lessons from Pope Francis's own relationships with his shapeholders in the coming sections, we must understand that Francis himself is turning into a shapeholder of the business environment. Even if he might sound like a negative shapeholder—like the voice of a prophet at the gates—it is a mistake to think that Francis is hostile to legitimate business interests (Calleja, 2014). As he clearly affirms in LS:

3 All papal interventions can be found at www.vatican.va

> Business is a noble vocation, directed to producing wealth and improving our world. It can be a fruitful source of prosperity for the areas in which it operates, especially if it sees the creation of jobs as an essential part of its service to the common good (LS, 129).

LS is a long and complex text that we cannot summarize here. It amounts to an urgent call for a deep cultural and spiritual change in "lifestyles and models of production and consumption" (LS, 59). It advances ideas and policies to confront an urgent crisis of the climate which affects primarily the less well-off. LS is driven by a sense of opportunity provided by the Climate Summit of December 2015. Let us consider particularly two principles that structure the Encyclical: the idea of a cultural revolution, which demands much more than policy changes, and intends to give shape to habits and culture; and the concept of integral development, or human ecology as the normative principle for this revolution.

A cultural revolution

LS challenges businesses to think broadly when defining its purpose. LS is not simply a repository of nice words and political makeup. Francis proposes to "move forward in a bold cultural revolution" (LS, 114). Quoting an Orthodox Christian Patriarch, Francis underlines the "ethical and spiritual roots of environmental problems, which require that we look for solutions not only in technology but in a change of humanity; otherwise we would be dealing merely with symptoms" (LS, 9). At the root of contemporary disorders, Francis signals a misguided "anthropocentrism" (LS, 115-121) that has led to a "technocratic paradigm" (LS, 107-108), by which mankind sees in nature—and by extension in people—raw material for manipulation through the power of technology.

Francis observes, "It has become countercultural to choose a lifestyle whose goals are even partly independent of technology, of its costs and its power to globalize and make us all the same" (LS, 108). However, he suggests this countercultural lifestyle might be become a growing trend:

> Liberation from the dominant technocratic paradigm does in fact happen sometimes ... An authentic humanity, calling for a new synthesis, seems to dwell in the midst of our technological culture, almost unnoticed, like a mist seeping gently beneath a closed door (LS, 112).

As opposed to consumerism and what he calls "the throwaway culture" (LS, 22)—connected with the "tyranny of relativism" (LS, 23)—Francis proposes a renewed attention to the climate as a "common good"—which should be administered and cultivated responsibly—and as a source of wisdom (LS, 123). Further on he fosters lifestyles that are rooted in communitarian bonds, human experiences of sharing, care for the poor and the needy, attention to culture and arts, etc. (LS, 222-223; 232).

For business this is a challenge. Big corporations are identified in the collective imagination with self-serving bureaucratic organizations, following technocratic thinking. Corporate interests are often perceived to be in conflict with local communities, family balance, intrinsically valuable work, moderate consumption, etc.

At the same time, the kind of futuristic fascination with hi-tech companies that was typical of certain cultures of the 20th-century is certainly still present—and we see it in popular attention to Apple product releases, or more recently in Tesla's automatic car. However, the new sensibility (Llano, 1991) demands that products and companies are ecology-friendly, but also community friendly, appealing in their marketing to a sense of proportion and fullness of life that is incompatible with compulsive consumption or unhealthy habits.

Business reputation in this field is weak. Within the current framing of the question, the burden of the proof lies on the side of business. The slightest mistake makes it to the news—not to mention systematic violations of regulations or socially irresponsible behaviour like that of Volkswagen which took a $7.27 billion charge to earnings and lost $26 billion in market value two days after the US Environmental Protection Agency (EPA) alleged the company used software to circumvent emission standards (KHQ, 2015).

People are reluctant to believe in a narrative of business that contradicts deeply rooted prejudices. And this is not a matter of one business in particular: it affects entire economic sectors, nationalities, and even the concept of a multinational corporation as such. This is therefore a collective challenge in shaping narratives.

Integral development and human ecology

Two central concepts in LS are the conception of "integral human development" and human ecology. Integral human development—introduced by Paul VI (Populorum Progressio, 14), and advanced by Pope Benedict XVI—"takes in not only the environment but also life, sexuality, marriage, the family, social relations" (Caritas in Veritate, 51) and goes further than just measuring GDP. In the same way, "human ecology" emphasizes that there is a natural order in human relationships that constitutes a limit to technocratic manipulation and market exchange.

In this direction, the crucial contribution of business to the common good and integral human development is—for Francis and Catholic Social Teaching since Leo XIII's Rerum Novarum in 1891—human work, under the principle of the priority of labour over capital (Sison and Frontrodona, 2012; Tablan, 2015). Labour rights have a structural dimension, but even more important is the cultural perception of business being on the side of workers (LS, 129).

The priority "should not be that technological progress increasingly replaces human work, for this would be detrimental to humanity. Work is a necessity, part of the meaning of life on this earth, a path to growth, human development and personal fulfilment" (LS, 128). This principle points to the much debated risk that technological disruption may end in massive unemployment (Ford, 2015). Work stability, permanent training, and decent retirement policies should be a concern for business leaders because, "to stop investing in people, in order to gain greater short-term financial gain, is bad business for society"

(LS, 128) and as current political conditions suggest, hampers the advance of a pro-business policy agenda.

To foster human ecology and integral development, Francis also stresses the importance of local cultures against a homogeneous globalization. This suggests local stakeholders should be more than just passive actors in designing products and services, or in contributing to shaping urban areas (LS, 150-153). The very notion of "quality of life" has to be enculturated, and cannot "be imposed from without, for quality of life must be understood within the world of symbols and customs proper to each human group" (LS, 144).

Of course, integral development needs to be sustainable development. But this, concludes Francis, "involves new forms of growth" (LS, 193). In a bold rejection of Keynesian economics and traditional commercial thinking, Francis suggests that "the time has come to accept decreased growth in some parts of the world, in order to provide resources for other places to experience healthy growth" (LS, 193). Shortly after, he affirms that it is necessary to go beyond "talk of sustainable growth" usually developed "into the categories of finance and technocracy", where "social and environmental responsibility of businesses often gets reduced to a series of marketing and image-enhancing measures" (LS, 194). Francis says business needs to walk the talk and grow more than their bottom lines.

Perhaps most challenging for business, Francis strongly denounces "the principle of the maximization of profits" as the ultimate purpose of business. He adds pressure on business to address societal concerns. In his opinion, "[this principle] frequently isolated from other considerations, reflects a misunderstanding of the very concept of the economy". If we follow just that rule, "little concern is given to whether it is at the cost of future resources or the health of the environment" (LS, 195). Businesses need to integrate reasonably their economic demands for efficiency, regulated by profit in the market, and their contribution to the common good, incorporating long-term considerations. This attitude might imply "a decrease in the pace of production and consumption", which could "give rise to another form of progress and development". These "efforts to promote a sustainable use of natural resources are not a waste of money, but rather an investment capable of providing other economic benefits in the medium term" (LS, 191).

Align

Let us now consider each of the steps for effective shapeholder engagement, relevant insights from LS, contrasting Francis's response with those by business in promoting free enterprise in the current crisis of trust in that principle.

It is both necessary and beneficial for a company to *align* towards a mission that delivers both profit and societal benefit. Effective engagement requires credibility with shapeholders. Given the history of businesses engaging with non-market forces in a tactical, disingenuous manner, there is an understandable scepticism that must be overcome. This makes enhancing authenticity with shapeholders by effectively aligning towards a unified purpose essential. In a word this demands identifying a truly *common* good (Pieper, 1966; Calleja and Melé, 2016).

Aligning authentically

Authentically aligning includes ensuring that all public commitments are fulfilled. Whatever purpose benefiting profit and society a company commits to, it must follow through. This…

> …not only includes good management practices, but governance structures and policies that guarantee that legal and ethical requirements are also observed in a company's day-to-day business, or voluntary occasional philanthropic engagement that might assist governmental efforts in the fields of social development or environmental protection (Aßländer and Curbach, 2014).

It is vital to actually *be* what one wants to *appear* being. And *being* goes beyond making statements and developing corporate social responsibility or CSR programmes. It demands creating a corporate culture that fosters virtues, running organizations with a sense of mission that transcends—without necessarily damaging, perhaps even supplementing—the bottom line, looking beyond maximizing quarterly profits to prioritize long-term considerations (Gassner, 2015).

Francis aligns

Cardinal Borgoglio made his purpose clear from the very outset. Even though the first Jesuit Pope, he embraced the name of the founder of the Franciscan Order—Francis of Assisi. Francis is famous for his concern for the poor and his love of nature, considering animals as his "brothers and sisters", preaching to birds. Borgoglio's embrace of Francis perfectly aligned with his intent to be a champion for the poor and the planet. Francis authentically adopted the spirit of Francis by his "no frills" approach including joining the cardinal bus in moving within the Vatican, paying his rent at the guest-house, turning off lights before leaving his working rooms, or forsaking the Apostolic Palace to live in the Vatican guesthouse (although he explained later he did this for "psychological reasons", for he needs to be with people).

All this has given Francis the attention of global public opinion and leaders in regards to the economy and the poor. Business people are likely to view Pope Francis's comments as representing "a caricature of market economics" (Rocca, 2015). Yet, let us remember, economics is not Francis's gig or his purpose and he lacks the experience of a real market economy (Lesley, 2015). One cannot deny that he has been very effective in advancing his purpose, calling attention to the consequences of our economic actions on the environment and the poorest among us, even if his understanding of the market economy sometimes does reflect his experience with cronyism in Argentina (Gregg, 2015).

Business inadequately aligns

In contrast, most business leaders can at best communicate in "caricatures" when addressing the plight of the needy. Their gig is market economics. If business leaders were half as good at advocating for the benefits of the market as Francis is at highlighting the needs of the poor, we would not have a vacuum of economic understanding that demagogues on the left and right fill with ill-informed prescriptions that will, arguably, be detrimental to citizens and businesses alike.

Some business people might suggest that aligning authentically to fulfilling a purpose that benefits both society and the bottom line of your enterprise is easier for an organization whose bottom line is saving souls. But they fail to stress, for instance, that it was the embrace of more capitalistic principles in China and India that has lifted hundreds of millions of people out of poverty in recent decades.

By finding new and creative ways to offer products and services that might satisfy the needs of larger sectors of the world population, companies can advance both their economic interest, and the common good, and be able to engage positively with shapeholders and stakeholders. Recycling, sustainable agriculture, new forms of cooperation and community organization protecting small producers, are examples of new business models that contribute to sustainability. A very concrete proposal of LS is the practice of environmental impact assessment before planning business (LS, 183).

Anticipate

In this hyper connected world it is imperative for companies to *anticipate* shapeholder concerns to either pre-empt them or address them in a timely and thoughtful manner before they begin to go viral. This not only helps a company to be prepared if it is assaulted by political or activist actions; it can also often shed light on actions the company can take to eliminate vulnerabilities and address legitimate concerns. The key is to be able to expect the unexpected. Along with exploring downside risks, a company should be on the lookout for upside opportunities to create shared value.

In order to promote the structural changes necessary to achieve the cultural revolution Francis seeks, Francis in LS relies on social activism more than on top-down bureaucratic reform: "local individuals and groups can make a real difference" (LS, 179). In particular their activism is necessary: "because the enforcement of laws is at times inadequate due to corruption". Thus: "public pressure has to be exerted in order to bring about decisive political action". "Unless citizens control political power—national, regional and municipal—it will not be possible to control damage to the environment" (LS, 179).

Businesses should not only anticipate this activism that Francis promotes. They should regularly dialogue with activists on their concerns. There is no better way to anticipate challenges coming your way. Activists will give you plenty of input, some of which you may find useful. For example, in LS Francis had specific ideas on energy production and consumption:

> forms of industrial production with maximum energy efficiency and diminished use of raw materials, removing from the market products which are less energy efficient or more polluting, improving transport systems, and encouraging the construction and repair of buildings aimed at reducing their energy consumption and levels of pollution (LS, 180).

Francis anticipates

It was not hard for Francis to recognize the challenges the Church faced. The prolonged sexual abuse scandal has been debilitating to the Church's reputation. Yet, Francis also anticipated the opportunity to address the economic angst that preoccupied the moment. Unlike politicians who appealed to people's darker instincts or offered utopian largesse, Francis perceived the opportunity to call on our better angels, asking us to elevate our concerns for the truly needy and our shared home, which he did with the publication of LS. Certainly, Francis's vision of capitalism is negatively influenced by his context. The World Economic Forum ranks Francis's Argentina among the three worst countries in corporate ethics, ranking it 138 out of 140 countries considered (World Economic Forum, 2016).

Business fails to anticipate

Business as a whole failed to foresee how this economic angst would unfavourably shape the makeup of the governing authorities that set the rules of commerce. They also never anticipated how allowing the brand of free enterprise to be tarnished by corruption would inform the view of world leaders who would set the tune to which they must march.

Assess

In order to determine the appropriate response to opportunities and risks posed by shapeholders, it is necessary to *assess* both the legitimacy of the concern or chance to collaborate and the prospects that the company's preferred position could prevail. Only then can a company determine whether the best action is to advance mutual interests, avert unworkable regulations, acquiesce to demands, or assemble a winning strategy and team to challenge shapeholder concerns or advance a worthy cause.

Francis accurately assesses

While Francis seemingly rightly assessed that concerns over the Church's poor performance in responding to sexual abuse scandals were legitimate and that though the situation offered little upside, the need to mitigate damage to both those who suffered and the Church's reputation was urgent. He also rightly assessed that speaking out strongly for those being left behind by economic and environmental trends was a legitimate concern shared by both the Church and many in society.

Business inaccurately assesses

Businesses on their side have failed to grasp that it is in their interests to ensure that the fruits of free enterprise are dispersed widely, disruptions caused by technology and globalization are mitigated, and corruption is confronted. They underestimated the cost that neglecting these imperatives would impose on them, by just repeating the mantras of trickle-down economics.

Due to their neglect, the business community's positive priorities—like the continued expansion of trade liberalization—have stalled, while negative consequences have mushroomed in terms of excessive regulations, inefficient government attempts at redistribution pressuring the need for higher taxes, and corruption limiting opportunities in emerging markets.

Avert/Acquiesce

If a company cannot prevail against a shapeholder claim or finds it unbeneficial, it should *avert* worse outcomes by enacting pre-emptive measures on legitimate claims. Even with illegitimate claims, if the cost of acting is inconsequential relative to fighting, perhaps it makes sense to *acquiesce* is some way. A delay in addressing legitimate claims reduces the benefit of company action while increasing the penalty the company would incur if forced to act later.

Francis averts further damage on sex scandal

Pope Francis recognized that the Church's response to its sexual abuse scandal undermined its credibility for addressing the needs of the disadvantaged. He understood that past inaction has caused a crisis of trust in the Church, and in ecclesiastical governance in particular, provoked by the continuing story of child abuse by catholic priests and the lack of transparency and accountability in dealing with this tragedy by the bishops and the Holy See itself.

Being merciful to priests put innocents at risk. Francis averted further harm to both the Church's credibility and those who suffered by taking concrete steps to change this travesty. While his work is still very much a work in process,

Francis set up a sex abuse commission comprising mostly lay people and acted on their recommendation to set up a tribunal to hold bishops to account (Breslow, 2015).

Francis continued the efforts of Pope Benedict and appointed a committee with a well-known champion in this fight as its head, Cardinal O'Malley from Boston. The committee also includes lay people and former victims of abuse. This part of the reform is also facing trouble. Recently a member resigned claiming that nothing serious is going on and the procedure for making bishops accountable in this regard—arguably the most relevant step so far—has not been put to use due to technical and political problems. However, just by showing commitment and being proactive, Pope Francis has managed to surf that wave and make it part of the positive narrative that surrounds him, averting further trust deterioration (Allen, 2015).

Business fails to avert

Businesses must recognize that forestalling populist action that would be economically disastrous for their companies and countries requires addressing the causes of economic uncertainty. They must more energetically combat market-distorting corruption, not just by avoiding corrupt conduct. They must also challenge it head on, even if doing so puts short-term economic prospects in a particular country like Argentina at risk.

Committing to standards of conduct like the Global Compact and sustainability goals addressing the United Nation's Sustainable Development Goals (SDGs) are merely first steps. More must be done to address underlying sources of economic uncertainty by promoting skills updating, financial literacy, healthy life and consumption styles, retirement saving and flourishing human communities. Companies must be attuned to how collaborating with NGOs, impact investing and for-benefit companies can benefit both their operations and the underprivileged by truly embracing the SDGs.

Advance and assemble

Business leaders must do more than ensuring their individual organizations' activities align with society in pursuit of a mutually beneficial purpose. They must also ensure that free enterprise delivers and is viewed by the public as delivering positive benefits for the many, not just the few. Francis *advanced* mutual interests for the Church and society by championing the concerns of the less fortunate. This was not only true to his purpose of fixating like his namesake on the poor and the planet, but also benefited society as it aided in the Church's efforts to preach a gospel of love.

In many places, corporations are well positioned to exert pressure or provide resources to public institutions, or to civic groups, for the common good, as *citoyens* (citizens) (Aßländer and Curbach, 2014). Political activism can be an extraordinary exercise of citizenship when it is directed towards not just the interests of top executives, but those of all the firm's constituencies, when it is seeking to advance the rule of law, formality in rulemaking and transparency.

In promoting a new economic model, business might have an active role, or on the contrary, wait for state regulations to impose it. The only way to guarantee a positive public attitude towards business is to be proactive, and to abide by the law transparently while at the same time going beyond the law. In Francis's words: "to claim economic freedom while real conditions bar many people from actual access to it, and while possibilities for employment continue to shrink, is to practice a doublespeak which brings politics", in our case, business, "into disrepute" (LS, 129).

In LS businesses are perceived as having the same short-term logic as governments. Is this necessarily so? Businesses by their own conduct either affirm or refute his suspicion. Francis includes consumers among the groups that should be active in social change (LS, 206). What could be done by business to engage with this group of stakeholders in a more positive way? One way is promoting ecological education in

> ...avoiding the use of plastic and paper, reducing water consumption, separating refuse, cooking only what can reasonably be consumed, showing care for other living beings, using public transport or car-pooling, planting trees, turning off unnecessary lights, or any number of other practices (LS, 211).

This active role of business in promoting the common good as an exercise of corporate social responsibility should be ruled by the principle of subsidiarity, a complementary principle to solidarity and the common good in Catholic Social Teaching, also mentioned in LS (Fort, 1996; Kelly, 2004). This normative role of subsidiarity in corporate citizenship has been recently emphasized by Aßländer and Curbach (2014).

In a word, it is necessary to *assemble* a strategy for prevailing, including forming a coalition of allies with common cause to ensure success if a confrontation results or a company seeks to advance a positive action. Prevailing in such face-offs requires optimizing *why, what, where, who* and *how*. Francis was not content to just have the Church directly address the needs of the poor and the planet. He assembled to engage in the arena of public opinion to prod individuals and government alike to pay more attention to their needs. He deftly managed the right mix of why, what, where, who, how, and when. In their feeble attempts to promote free enterprise commercial actors have not. Let's explore in more detail what could this mean in practice.

Why

Public engagement is most effective when you have a clear answer for why you are engaging. This is best when your "why" is aligned with your purpose that harmonizes the organization's bottom line and societal benefit.

For Francis, everything is focused on the least among us and the home we share. This bolsters his effectiveness.

Companies would be equally effective if they genuinely embraced the "why" of unleashing capitalism's unmatched ability to generate and equitably distribute wealth. Here capitalism is meant as "an economic system which recognizes the fundamental and positive role of business, the market, private property and the resulting responsibility for the means of production, as well as free human creativity in the economic sector" (*Centessimus Annus, 42*). Yet business behaviour betrays the opposite. The accumulation of evidence suggests that not only are corporations not earnest in addressing distortions in the conduct of free enterprise in international markets, they are busy erecting further barriers in America (*The Economist*, 2016).

For companies to deserve less disdain, they must accept more antitrust oversight, be sincere in pushing to simplify regulations, be sceptical about licensing schemes, and direct their lobbying efforts towards levelling the playing field, not tilting it. The acid test of a company's sincerity in the United States is whether it supports comprehensive tax reform where all companies and industries forfeit their special benefits to lower the rate for all.

What

Francis set forth the question, "Are we conducting our Church, economic, and environmental affairs in a manner that discharges our duties to help those most in need?" This question directed his pivot on the Church's approach to sexual abuse to those who suffered. It salvaged an inept global effort to promote climate change action from less animating questions like, "do you want the seas to rise?" to more compelling questions like "how can you in good conscious not act when most who are disadvantaged by rising seas are the poorest people on the planet?"

Businesses seem fixated on a question of "what is best for business" instead of "what delivers the most sustainable and equitably distributed prosperity for all?" Few care about the first question. Only if commercial activities are an adequate answer to the second question will their licence to operate be renewed.

Where

What is perhaps most revolutionary in Francis's approach to engagement is his changing the venue of where issues are debated and decided. The United States and its allies reshaped the world order after the Second World War, setting up an Atlantic-centric global governance system which tends to ignore peripheral phenomena. Francis's voice is amplified by the fact that today's economic angst reflects concern by the people that while the economy has become global, there is no effective watchful eye to ensure that commerce is being done in a way that benefits all. The Dickensian abuses of the United Kingdom largely resulted from businesses rising to a national scale while the locus of political power remained local. The people are demanding a global economic watchdog if we are to continue towards integrating the world's economies. Pope Francis is filling that void. At his recent address to the UN Francis suggested that without "…interventions on the international level, mankind would not have been able to survive the unchecked use of its own possibilities" (Francis, 2015b).

It is in companies' best interest to seek to fill the vacuum of global regulation that fuels Francis's appeal. Not only would this give consumers and workers more confidence that the rules of commerce are fair, it could also prevent companies from being disadvantaged by heavy handed governments. The World Trade Organization's global standards and dispute resolution system provide a model that it would be wise for businesses to consider for application to other aspects of global concern.

Who

In many cases, Francis has been the primary spokesperson for the Church. The coalition he seeks to yield is not just faithful Catholics, but those of many religious persuasions, with a special appeal to those who feel left behind by the modern economy. The audiences of Francis's advocacy have varied based on the topic. In relation to the sexual abuse scandal, he seeks to both persuade the actions of church leadership and regain the confidence of parishioners and the public. In regard to the impact of environmental and economic policy on the poor, he seeks to target both governing authorities and the conduct of businesses by influencing personal choices or citizens and encouraging them to engage.

When defending free enterprise, it is those closest to whatever blast furnace drives your enterprise that will be your most effective spokespersons. A CEO can more easily capture media attention, but passionate stakeholders or shapeholders are more likely to convince sceptics. A coalition needs to begin with your stakeholders, but also include the shapeholders with whom you have collaborated. An audience is whoever holds the keys to either unleash or muzzle the power of markets. The lack of success of Honeywell's CEO David Coates in organizing a Fix the Debt organization and campaign reflects the greater difficulty for modern day CEOs to address society's most pressing issues (Fix the Debt, 2016). Businesses have fared little better in promoting trade liberalization: no 2016 candidate for US President supports the Trans Pacific Partnership agreement. They need to build bigger coalitions if they are to succeed in any of these efforts.

How

While Francis has used a communication channel unique to popes with his recent encyclical to carry his message, he has also taken advantage of many other communications channels. In an effort to better connect the Church with millennials, three years ago Francis joined Twitter (Griffith, 2015). More recently he has embraced Instagram (Stack, 2016).

Yet, perhaps the most impactful way Francis uses to get his message out is to travel, using locations as a springboard to constantly infuse concern for the needs of the poor into the consciousness of the world. Understanding that tangible messages are the most impactful, Francis has practised what some call "a culture of encounter", meeting people suffering injustice where they are. In Bolivia, he visited a notorious prison, not only to highlight the need to address overcrowding, an unresponsive justice system, and the lack of training opportunities, but also to affirm the dignity of all prisoners (Francis, 2015a). In Nairobi, Kenya he visited a slum to point out the inequality and injustice of what he called a "new form of colonialism" that exacerbates the "dreadful injustice of urban exclusion" (Francis, 2015c). With all these symbolic gestures he captures the imagination and generates a narrative that is deeply rooted, making his figure nearly impossible to attack, and his failures or mistakes overlooked, as Vaticanist John Allen often points out.

Just as Francis makes the case for the plight of the poor on a continuous basis in very tangible ways like visiting prisons and slums, so must business make the case for free enterprise on a year in, year out basis, by making the tangible benefits of open markets and the real costs of market distortions visible to everyday citizens. However, business engagement on this front is usually limited to engaging legislators, and then only when specific legislation is up for a vote.

When

Effective public engagement requires careful timing as to when you engage on issues. While Francis maintained a steady drumbeat promoting his concern for the poor and the planet, he skilfully timed his crescendos, publishing Laudato Si to impact the 2015 Paris Climate Summit and likely timing his visit to the Mexican border to highlight a humane approach to immigrants during a time of great debate on the subject during the 2016 US Presidential Primaries.

In a similar way, businesses must always conduct themselves in a manner that testifies to the benefits of markets, yet be prepared to join together with its expanded coalition to affront attacks on capitalism's efficacy or advance the reach of its benefits, such as with trade agreements that remove barriers to trade.

Conclusion

Business leaders should learn from Francis how to engage with shapeholders, to avoid conflicts and misunderstandings and be able to advance the common good, which includes better conditions for business, so they can deliver benefits to society. This can be done in two ways: first, learning from the Pope the attitudes and strategies in relating with political, regulatory, media and activist actors whose actions are so influential in business performance, and ultimately in business contribution to the common good. Second, by reading Francis they might discover future cultural trends which will lead to social demands on companies, and should orient the exercise of corporate citizenship. A way of doing this is reading and implementing the encyclical of Francis on the environment and integral human development, which points to a veritable cultural revolution.

It is in their own interests that businesses show that they are part of the solution, and not a central part of the problem, as they are seen today. But this aim can only be attained by sound diagnosis and real commitment. A purely cosmetic reputation campaign is not going to regain public trust in business, and could make things even worse. A strategy like this is a moral imperative for exercising corporate citizenship constructively as well as a long-term winning strategy in purely economic terms.

References

Aßländer, M.S., & Curbach, J. (2014). The corporation as citoyen? Towards a new understanding of corporate citizenship. *Journal of Business Ethics*, 120, 541-554.

Benedict XVI (2009). *Encyclical Letter "Caritas in Veritate"*. Vatican City: Vatican Press.

Breslow, J.M. (2015). The Vatican after Francis: Has the Pope met his mandate for change? *Frontline*. Retrieved from: http://www.pbs.org/wgbh/frontline/article/the-vatican-after-francis-has-the-pope-met-his-mandate-for-change/

Calleja, R. (2014). Pope Francis: Knockin' on markets' doors. *Business Ethics Blog Network*. Retrieved from: http://blog.iese.edu/ethics/2014/07/10/pope-francis-knockin-on-markets-doors/

Calleja, R., & Melé, D. (2016). Political wisdom in management and corporate governance. *Philosophy of Management*, 15(2), 99-119.

Economist (2016, March 26). Too much of a good thing. *Economist*. Retrieved from: http://www.economist.com/news/briefing/21695385-profits-are-too-high-america-needs-giant-dose-competition-too-much-good-thing

Fix the Debt (2016). David Cote. *Fix the Debt*. Retrieved from: http://www.fixthedebt.org/david-cote

Ford, M. (2015). *Rise of the Robots: Technology and the Threat of a Jobless Future*. New York: Basic Books.

Fort, T.L. (1996). Business as mediating institutions. *Business Ethics Quarterly*, 6(2), 149-163.

Francis I (2015). *Encyclical letter "Laudato Si": On Care for Our Common Home*. Vatican City: Vatican Press. Retrieved from: http://w2.vatican.va/content/francesco/en/encyclicals/documents/papa-francesco_20150524_enciclica-laudato-si.html

Francis I (2015a, July 10). *Visit to Santa Cruz-Pamasola Rehabilitation Center: Address of the Holy Father*. Retrieved from: https://w2.vatican.va/content/francesco/en/speeches/2015/july/documents/papa-francesco_20150710_bolivia-palmasola.html

Francis I (2015b, September 25). *Meeting with the Members of the General Assembly of the United Nations Organization: Address of the Holy Father*. Retrieved from: http://w2.vatican.va/content/francesco/en/speeches/2015/september/documents/papa-francesco_20150925_onu-visita.html

Francis I (2015c, November 27). *Visit to Kangemi Slum: Address of his Holiness Pope Francis*. Retrieved from: http://w2.vatican.va/content/francesco/en/speeches/2015/november/documents/papa-francesco_20151127_kenya-kangemi.html

Gassner, L. (2015). *Mission Driven: Moving from Profit to Purpose*. Boise, ID: Elevate.

Gregg, S. (2015). Laudato Si: Well intentioned, economically flawed. *Policy*, 31(2), 49-51.

Griffith, E. (2015, September 15). Inside the Pope's social media plan to win over millennials. *Fortune.* Retrieved from: http://fortune.com/2015/09/15/pope-francis-social-media/

John Paul II (1991). *Encyclical letter "Centesimus Annus".* Vatican City: Vatican Press. Retrieved from: http://w2.vatican.va/content/john-paul-ii/en/encyclicals/documents/hf_jp-ii_enc_01051991_centesimus-annus.html

Kell, G., Kingo, L., & Reynolds, F. (2015, August 7). *Open Letter to His Holiness Pope Francis from the United Nations Global Compact Responding to Laudato Si.* Retrieved from: https://www.unglobalcompact.org/docs/issues_doc/Environment/Laudato_Si_Open_Letter_UN_Global_Compact.pdf

Kelly, J. (2004). Solidarity and subsidiarity: "Organizing principles" for corporate moral leadership in the new global economy. *Journal of Business Ethics,* 52(3), 283-295.

Kennedy, M. (2013). Social media provides a megaphone for organizations intent on shaping the corporate environment. *Strategy and Leadership,* 41(5), 39-47.

Kennedy, M. (2016). *Seven Steps for Shapeholder Success.* Retrieved from: http://www.markkennedy.com/7a-shapeholder-engagement.html

KHQ (2015, September 22). VW loses $26 billion in market value in 2 days. *KHQ.* Retrieved from: http://www.khq.com/story/30091348/vw-loses-26-billion-in-market-value-in-2-days

Lesley, A. (2015, June 2). Rev. Martin Schlag thinks Pop Francis will appreciate American economy. *World Religion News.* Retrieved from: http://www.worldreligionnews.com/religion-news/christianity/rev-martin-schlag-thinks-pope-francis-will-appreciate-american-economy

Llano, A. (1991). *The New Sensibility.* Pamplona: Servicio de Publicaciones de la Universidad de Navarra.

Paul VI (1967). *Encyclical Letter "Populorum Progressio".* Vatican City: Vatican Press.

Pieper, J. (1966). *The Four Cardinal Virtues: Prudence, Justice, Fortitude, Temperance.* Notre Dame, IN: University of Notre Dame Press.

Reuters (2016, June 9). French court fines Uber for running illegal taxi service. *The Guardian.* Retrieved from: https://www.theguardian.com/technology/2016/jun/09/french-court-fines-uber-for-running-illegal-taxi-service

Rocca, F.X. (2015). Pope blames markets for environment's ills. *Wall Street Journal.* Retrieved from: http://www.wsj.com/articles/pope-delivers-powerful-message-on-climate-change-1434621606

Sison, A. (2009). From CSR to corporate citizenship: Anglo-American and continental European perspectives. *Journal of Business Ethics,* 3(89), 235-246.

Sison, A.J.G., & Fontrodona, J. (2012). The common good of the firm in the Aristotelian-Thomistic tradition. *Business Ethics Quarterly,* 31(2), 211-246.

Stack, L. (2016, March 19). Get ready, internet. The Pope has joined Instagram. *New York Times.* Retrieved from: http://www.nytimes.com/2016/03/19/world/europe/pope-francis-instagram-franciscus.html?_r=0

Tablan, F. (2015). Catholic social teachings: Toward a meaningful work. *Journal of Business Ethics,* 128(2), 291-303.

Voelcker, J. (2010, July 8). California yanks Prius perks: No more lane access. *Green Car Reports.* Retrieved from: http://www.greencarreports.com/news/1046928_california-yanks-prius-perks-no-more-hybrid-hov-lane-access

World Economic Forum (2016). Argentina. *World Economic Forum.* Retrieved from: http://reports.weforum.org/global-competitiveness-report-2015-2016/economies/#economy=ARG

Zadek, S. (2004). The path to corporate responsibility. *Harvard Business Review,* 82(12), 125-132.

DOI: [10.9774/GLEAF.4700.2016.de.00011]

Corporate Support for the SDGs

A South African Perspective

Daniel Malan

University of Stellenbosch Business School, South Africa

The Sustainable Development Goals (SDGs) were adopted by the United Nations General Assembly on 25 September 2015 along with the 2030 Agenda for Sustainable Development. Although led by member states, the post-2015 development agenda encourages the private sector to support the SDGs in partnership with governments and civil society. Historically, this support would form part of more traditional (philanthropic) corporate responsibility programmes, but increasingly such corporate activities are viewed as strategic ways to create value. A common problem with universal goals is that they do not provide enough local context and hence their pursuit does not provide meaningful impact at the local level. With reference to Integrative Social Contracts Theory it is argued that universal goals can be more meaningful when interpreted as a hypothetical macro contract, while at the same time supported by practical activities that take the local context into account (micro contracts). The most recent sustainability reports and Communications on Progress (COPs) of South African companies who are active participants in the United Nations Global Compact (UNGC) were analysed in order to assess their support for the SDGs. Although not empirically verifiable, it is postulated that the low levels of disclosure by South African corporations indicate a lack of engagement with important societal issues.

- Sustainable Development Goals
- National Development Plan
- United Nations Global Compact
- Integrative Social Contracts Theory

Daniel Malan is a Senior Lecturer in Ethics and Governance and Director of the Centre for Corporate Governance in Africa at the University of Stellenbosch Business School in South Africa. His focus areas are corporate governance, business ethics and corporate responsibility. He is a member of the following initiatives: the World Economic Forum's Global Agenda Council on Values, the International Corporate Governance Network's Integrated Business Reporting Committee and the Anti-Corruption Working Group of the United Nations Principles for Responsible Management Education (PRME). He is also a portfolio partner at the International Centre for Corporate Governance at the University of St Gallen. Previously he was an associate director with KPMG Forensic, where he was responsible for ethics and integrity services. His educational qualifications include a PhD in Business Administration, a Master's degree in Philosophy as well as a Master's degree in Business Administration (MBA), all from the University of Stellenbosch in South Africa. He lives in Stellenbosch with his wife and two daughters, where he is the residential head of Wilgenhof, the oldest university men's residence in Africa.

✉ PO Box 610, Bellville, 7535 South Africa

🖳 daniel.malan@usb.ac.za

N 2015 WORLD LEADERS COMMITTED to the Sustainable Development Goals (SDGs),[1] a global initiative to achieve sustainable development. The 17 Sustainable Development Goals were adopted at the United Nations (UN) in New York on 25 September 2015 in a global context that is increasingly characterized by concerns about social inequality, conflict and climate change. The official UN resolution refers to the SDGs as "a historic decision on a comprehensive, far-reaching and people-centred set of universal and transformative Goals and targets" (United Nations, 2015, p. 3), and further states that "eradicating poverty in all its forms and dimensions, including extreme poverty, is the greatest global challenge and an indispensable requirement for sustainable development" (United Nations, 2015, p. 3). The essence of the SDGs is captured in the following statement (United Nations, 2015, p. 3):

> We resolve, between now and 2030, to end poverty and hunger everywhere; to combat inequalities within and among countries; to build peaceful, just and inclusive societies; to protect human rights and promote gender equality and the empowerment of women and girls; and to ensure the lasting protection of the planet and its natural resources. We resolve also to create conditions for sustainable, inclusive and sustained economic growth, shared prosperity and decent work for all, taking into account different levels of national development and capacities.

The 17 SDGs are described by the UN as "integrated and indivisible" (United Nations, 2015, p. 6) and are presented in Table 1.

Table 1 Sustainable Development Goals

Goal 1	End poverty in all its forms everywhere
Goal 2	End hunger, achieve food security and improved nutrition and promote sustainable agriculture
Goal 3	Ensure healthy lives and promote well-being for all at all ages
Goal 4	Ensure inclusive and equitable quality education and promote lifelong learning opportunities for all
Goal 5	Achieve gender equality and empower all women and girls
Goal 6	Ensure availability and sustainable management of water and sanitation for all
Goal 7	Ensure access to affordable, reliable, sustainable and modern energy for all

Continued

---

1 The SDGs replaced the Millennium Development Goals (MDGs). In 2000 world leaders committed to the global goal of "eliminating extreme poverty", by signing the Millennium Declaration at the UN Millennium Summit. The Declaration laid out eight MDGs with the aim of achieving them by 2015: 1) eradicate extreme poverty and hunger; 2) achieve universal primary education; 3) promote gender equality and empower women; 4) reduce child mortality; 5) improve maternal health; 6) combat HIV/AIDS, malaria and other diseases; 7) ensure environmental sustainability; and 8) develop a global partnership for development (United Nations, 2000).

Goal 8	Promote sustained, inclusive and sustainable economic growth, full and productive employment and decent work for all
Goal 9	Build resilient infrastructure, promote inclusive and sustainable industrialization and foster innovation
Goal 10	Reduce inequality within and among countries
Goal 11	Make cities and human settlements inclusive, safe, resilient and sustainable
Goal 12	Ensure sustainable consumption and production patterns
Goal 13	Take urgent action to combat climate change and its impacts
Goal 14	Conserve and sustainably use the oceans, seas and marine resources for sustainable development
Goal 15	Protect, restore and promote sustainable use of terrestrial ecosystems, sustainably manage forests, combat desertification, and halt and reverse land degradation and halt biodiversity loss
Goal 16	Promote peaceful and inclusive societies for sustainable development, provide access to justice for all and build effective, accountable and inclusive institutions at all levels
Goal 17	Strengthen the means of implementation and revitalize the global partnership for sustainable development

The UN calls on companies to contribute to realizing these goals through four channels: first and foremost, companies should demonstrate support through their core business activities. This includes the need for companies to operate in accordance with the ten UN Global Compact principles, discussed below. Second, it is expected that companies should support the principles through advocacy and public policy engagement activities. The third channel comprises the more traditional social investment and philanthropy activities, and finally companies are urged to engage in partnerships with other signatories or stakeholders through collective action. Companies are invited to make public commitments on an online platform, "Partnerships for SDGs", (United Nations, 2016) and to report annually against the targets set out in the commitment, either in their annual or sustainability (or equivalent) report.

The normative foundation of the SDGs

The repeated use of concepts like inclusivity, equality, justice and accountability in the SDGs illustrates the normative foundation of the SDGs. There is an explicit reference to the values of "peace, dialogue and international cooperation" which underpin the UN (United Nations, 2015, p. 12). This forms part of a larger debate about the normative foundation of development and the moral behaviour of organizations. Many would argue that, although the practical implications of an inability to address sustainable development challenges effectively are most convincing in a corporate environment, ultimately there is a moral component that cannot, and should not, be ignored (Goodpaster and Matthews, 1982; Kaptein and Wempe, 2002; Smurthwaite, 2008; Williams, 2014a). In his encyclical letter, Laudato Si, Pope Francis (2015) states the following: "Authentic human development has a moral character. It presumes full respect for the human person, but it must also be concerned for the world around us" (LS, 6).

Although Laudato Si is predominantly concerned with the environment, which is not the main focus of this paper, it is important to appreciate the integrated approach that is proposed by Pope Francis (2015): "we have to realize that a true ecological approach always becomes a social approach; it must integrate questions of justice in debates on the environment, so as to hear *both the cry of the earth and the cry of the poor*" (LS, 35).

Although Pope Francis has made an important contribution far beyond the borders of the Roman Catholic Church, it is acknowledged that the views of a religious leader might not always be sufficient to change the minds of business leaders. To influence the behaviour of business one should either convince them that moral character should be reflected in corporate behaviour, or that different behaviour will be more lucrative over the long term (the business case), or both. Historically, support for an initiative like the SDGs would form part of more traditional (philanthropic) corporate responsibility programmes, but increasingly such corporate activities are viewed as strategic ways to create value. This approach presents both opportunities and problems.

Porter and Kramer introduced the "big idea" of creating shared value (CSV)—connecting societal and economic progress, for example through reconceiving products and markets and redefining productivity in the value chain (Porter and Kramer, 2011):

> The concept of shared value ... recognizes that societal needs, not just conventional economic needs, define markets. It also recognizes that social harms or weaknesses frequently create **internal** costs for firms—such as wasted energy or raw materials, costly accidents, and the need for remedial training to compensate for inadequacies in education. And addressing societal harms and constraints does not necessarily raise costs for firms, because they can innovate through using new technologies, operating methods, and management approaches—and as a result, increase their productivity and expand their markets.

There is no doubt that this contribution of Porter and Kramer has been very influential in the corporate world (the main audience for the *Harvard Business Review*, in which the article was published), and to some extent also in the academic world. However, many questions have been asked about the originality of the contribution, as well as the desirability of the approach. It is interesting to consider—side by side in Table 2—the views of Porter and Kramer with those of Milton Friedman from his well-known and controversial article ("The social responsibility of business is to increase its profits") that was published in the *New York Times* in 1970.

Table 2 Comparison between the views of Porter & Kramer and Friedman

Porter & Kramer	Friedman
"It is not philanthropy but self-interested behavior to create economic value by creating societal value. If all companies individually pursued shared value connected to their particular businesses, society's overall interests would be served. And companies would acquire legitimacy in the eyes of the communities in which they operated". (Porter and Kramer, 2011, p. 17)	"It may well be in the long run interest of a corporation that is a major employer in a small community to devote resources to providing amenities to that community or to improving its government. That may make it easier to attract desirable employees, it may reduce the wage bill or lessen losses from pilferage and sabotage or have other worthwhile effects". (Friedman, 2002, p. 36)

A very hard-hitting critique of CSV was published in the *California Management Review* (Crane *et al.*, 2014). In summary, the authors describe the following shortcomings of CSV: "[I]t is unoriginal, it ignores the tensions between social and economic goals, it is naïve about the challenges of business compliance, and it is based on a shallow conception of the role of the corporation in society" (Crane *et al.*, 2014, p. 131). Ultimately, the authors argue, CSV is "a reactionary rather than transformational response to the crisis of capitalism" (Crane *et al.*, 2014, p. 131).

They do acknowledge the following strengths of CSV: it appeals to practitioners and scholars, it elevates social goals to a strategic level, it articulates a clear role for governments in responsible behaviour, and it adds rigour to the concept of "conscious capitalism" (Crane *et al.*, 2014, p. 132).

In their response to the article, Porter and Kramer state that they find it puzzling that the authors can acknowledge the wide and positive reception of the article, yet claim that it does not say anything new. They find this puzzling,

> ... especially given the substantial changes in behaviour in corporations around the world, both large and small, that have come as a direct result of the article. Clearly something about this article has moved companies to embrace the idea and act in ways that previous literature has not (Porter and Kramer, 2014, p. 149).

It is hard to believe that Porter and Kramer can make the error of logic of equating the "wide and positive reception" of the article with the novelty of the content. It is almost akin to stating that E.L. James must be a good author because *Fifty Shades of Grey* sold more than 100 million copies worldwide. Applying the same logic, surely James's book has also moved people to act in ways that previous literature has not.

Porter and Kramer respond briefly to some of the criticism in the article, using the defence that the *Harvard Business Review* does not allow footnotes and countering with the words "mistaken" and "utterly misses our point". Then the gloves come off:

> It is precisely the wishful thinking of writers like Mr Crane that has led to so many corporate responsibility and sustainability arguments falling on deaf corporate ears,

by insisting that profit-seeing (sic) enterprises need to abandon their core purpose for the sake of the greater good (Porter and Kramer, 2014: 150).

In their response, Crane and his co-authors accuse Porter and Kramer of presenting a "wilful caricature" of their "fairly nuanced position" and manage to get in the final stab: "Where the wishful thinking really comes in though is in Porter and Kramer's naïve belief that the role of business in addressing the world's major social problems can, or should, only be addressed through the lens of corporate self-interest" (Crane *et al.*, 2014, p. 152).

Waddock (2013, p. 43) places an emphasis on the limitations of the business case:

> As business leaders tackle sustainability, one thing is important to understand: not every action that needs to be taken to create a more sustainable world has what is commonly called a "business case". Some things simply need to be done as part of a precautionary approach, or because they are the right thing to do.

Of course, both sides have a point. It is impossible to deny the "Porter effect", even if one does not like it. Anything with Porter's name attached to it is bound to have a more immediate impact in the corporate world. Second, Porter does manage to address a corporate audience in non-academic language, which is essential if one wants to achieve traction and initiate action in the corporate world. Zollo and Mele (2013) put this eloquently. After having acknowledged that "Porter and Kramer's claim to novelty might be relatively weak", they go on to state the following:

> ... the fact that they could achieve with that one article what scores of academics failed to achieve in the course of decades of work goes entirely to their merit, and rings painful notes to the capacity of management scholars to influence practice with their research, teaching and collective "voice" in the core debates in our society (Zollo and Mele, 2013, pp. 19-20).

This is also the position of Georg Kell, former executive director of the UN Global Compact, who welcomed the contribution in very pragmatic terms:

> I am personally very delighted that Porter came out with this work because it had an impact on the US where the silly ideological debate between shareholder and stakeholder dominated the public domain. And the shared value notion helped to overcome this and put it in the right direction ... And if it takes a Harvard professor to mainstream the concept—great! But it is certainly not new. But it is most welcome.[2]

At the same time, the critique of Crane *et al.* (2014) is valid. However, a corporate audience does not concern itself with purported lack of originality and CEOs do not read footnotes. From a purely pragmatic point of view, if it is Porter's CSV that can get them to do certain things rather than strategic CSR, does it really matter?

---

2 Personal communication with Georg Kell, Executive Director, UN Global Compact, 5 August 2013.

There *is* a part that matters. The lack of a normative foundation in CSV brings one back to the business case versus the moral case debate. The "enlightened self-interest" approach is a problematic one because it only works up to a point.

There is always the realization that from time to time a corporation has to make decisions that will conflict with either its own self-interest or those of its stakeholders. It is easy to justify why bribery is wrong (even if you win the contract, you might go to jail) or why it is good to invest huge amounts of money in environmental technology not required by law (it will improve reputation and ultimately you will save money). It is not so easy if you have to decide whether to retrench employees, close plants or pay wages that do not conform to trade union demands.

This point is articulated eloquently by Crane *et al.* (2014, p. 136) in their critique of CSV: "While seeking win-win opportunities is clearly important, this does not provide guidance for the many situations where social and economic outcomes will not be aligned for all stakeholders".

There seems to be a perceived correlation between the moral case and philanthropy, and between the business case and strategic CSR. However, there is a need to decouple the *motivation* for specific behaviour from the behaviour itself. It is becoming increasingly clear that the most effective way for corporations to respond to societal expectations is to integrate these activities into their day-to-day activities, and not to manage these as something separate or peripheral. But doing it in a particular way has little to do with the motivation for doing it in the first place.

Corporations that want to make a contribution in the field of corporate responsibility and sustainable development have to negotiate two tensions: not only between the business and the moral case, but also between the global perspective and local application. Before the local application is analysed with reference to South Africa, the SDGs are discussed with reference to other initiatives.

The SDGs and other initiatives

It should be noted that the SDGs are not new, and in some respects could be regarded as a more comprehensive restatement of the MDGs. It is noteworthy that the most comprehensive expansion has been in the area of environmental sustainability, while previous goals relating to health and child mortality have been consolidated into one goal: to "ensure healthy lives and promote well-being for all at all ages". The use of the word "revitalise" with regards to the global partnership seems to suggest that this partnership was not effective during the MDG period. It is not clear why the reference to a global partnership had to be included as a *separate* goal. The need for one single partnership is not really helpful (unless it refers to collective support for the SDGs themselves, in which case it is circular), while the need for multiple partnerships is implicit in reaching all the other goals. For example, economic growth, employment and industrialization would not be possible without partnerships. Table 3 compares the eight MDGs to the expanded list of SDGs.

Table 3 Millennium Development Goals compared to the Sustainable Development Goals

Millennium Development Goals	Sustainable Development Goals (rearranged)
Eradicate extreme poverty and hunger	End poverty in all its forms everywhere End hunger, achieve food security and improved nutrition, and promote sustainable agriculture Reduce inequality within and among countries
Achieve universal primary education	Ensure inclusive and equitable quality education and promote lifelong learning opportunities for all
Promote gender equality and empower women	Achieve gender equality and empower all women and girls
Reduce child mortality Improve maternal health Combat HIV/AIDS, malaria and other diseases	Ensure healthy lives and promote well-being for all at all ages
Ensure environmental sustainability	Ensure availability and sustainable management of water and sanitation for all Ensure access to affordable, reliable, sustainable and modern energy for all Make cities and human settlements inclusive, safe, resilient and sustainable Ensure sustainable consumption and production patterns Take urgent action to combat climate change and its impacts Conserve and sustainably use the oceans, seas and marine resources for sustainable development Protect, restore and promote sustainable use of terrestrial ecosystems, sustainably manage forests, combat desertification, halt and reverse land degradation, and halt biodiversity loss

Continued

Millennium Development Goals	Sustainable Development Goals (rearranged)
Develop a Global Partnership for Development	Promote sustained, inclusive and sustainable economic growth, full and productive employment and decent work for all
	Build resilient infrastructure, promote inclusive and sustainable industrialization and foster innovation
	Promote peaceful and inclusive societies for sustainable development, provide access to justice for all, and build effective, accountable and inclusive institutions at all levels
	Strengthen the means of implementation and revitalise the global partnership for sustainable development

The United Nations Global Compact

The SDGs cannot be discussed from a corporate perspective without reference to the United Nations (UN) Global Compact. The UN Global Compact is the world's largest voluntary corporate citizenship initiative and used to describe itself as "a strategic policy initiative for businesses that are committed to aligning their operations and strategies with ten universally accepted principles in the areas of human rights, labour, environment and anti-corruption" (UNGC, 2013). The ten principles were derived from the Universal Declaration of Human Rights, the International Labour Organization's Declaration on Fundamental Principles and Rights at Work, the Rio Declaration on Environment and Development, and the United Nations Convention against Corruption. More recently this description has changed to that of a "voluntary initiative based on CEO commitments to implement universal sustainability principles and to take steps to support UN goals" (UNGC, 2016).

Table 4 maps the UN Global Compact principles against selected SDGs. All human rights-related principles are linked with SDG 16, while some of the SDGs addressing the basic human condition (e.g. poverty, hunger and health) cannot be linked to a specific UN Global Compact principle. Again, the global partnership goal (SDG 17) is so pervasive (and obsolete) that it cannot be linked to a specific principle.

Table 4 UN Global Compact mapped against SDGs

Principle	Description	Link with SDGs
Principle 1	Businesses should support and respect the protection of internationally proclaimed human rights	Peace, justice and strong institutions (16)
Principle 2	Businesses should make sure that they are not complicit in human rights abuses	Peace, justice and strong institutions (16)
Principle 3	Businesses should uphold the freedom of association and the effective recognition of the right to collective bargaining	Peace, justice and strong institutions (16)
Principle 4	Businesses should support the elimination of all forms of forced and compulsory labour	Decent work and economic growth (8)
Principle 5	Businesses should support the effective abolition of child labour	Peace, justice and strong institutions (16)
Principle 6	Businesses should support the elimination of discrimination in respect of employment and occupation	Gender equality (5) Reduced inequality (10)
Principle 7	Businesses should support a precautionary approach to environmental challenges	Climate action (13)
Principle 8	Businesses should undertake initiatives to promote greater environmental responsibility	Affordable and clean energy (7) Sustainable cities and communities (11) Responsible consumption and production (12)
Principle 9	Businesses should encourage the development and diffusion of environmentally friendly technologies	Industry, innovation and infrastructure (9) Clean water and sanitation (6)
Principle 10	Businesses should work against corruption in all its forms, including extortion and bribery	Peace, justice and strong institutions (16)

The UN Global Compact aims to engage business in innovative ways to mainstream the ten principles in business strategies and operations around the world and garner business support for UN goals and issues. Companies that become signatories are expected to implement the ten principles in their decision-making, strategy and operations, disclose their performance in an annual Communication on Progress (COP) and promote the principles in their day-to-day activities. Upon joining, companies are asked to make a regular annual financial contribution to the initiative (UNGC, 2016).

A symbiotic relationship exists between the UN SDGs and the UN Global Compact. The UN Global Compact initiative is not only aimed at promoting the ten universal principles, but also sets out to "catalyse business action in support of UN goals". Conversely, the SDGs cannot be reached without the involvement and contribution of the private sector, which is facilitated through the UN Global Compact.[3]

The SDGs explicitly refer to the role of the private sector in achieving the goals (United Nations, 2015, p. 29):

> Private business activity, investment and innovation are major drivers of productivity, inclusive economic growth and job creation. We acknowledge the diversity of the private sector, ranging from micro-enterprises to cooperatives to multinationals. We call upon all businesses to apply their creativity and innovation to solving sustainable development challenges.

Companies are invited to report on their support for the SDGs. In the words of Ban Ki-moon, then UN Secretary-General (quoted in Global Reporting Initiative, United Nations Global Compact, World Business Council on Sustainable Development, 2015a, p. 4): "Business is a vital partner in achieving the Sustainable Development Goals. Companies can contribute through their core activities, and we ask companies everywhere to assess their impact, set ambitious goals and communicate transparently about the results".

The Global Reporting Initiative, UN Global Compact and the World Business Council for Sustainable Development jointly developed the SDG Compass to guide companies on how to align, manage and measure their contribution to the SDGs. Five steps are recommended: understand the SDGs, define priorities, set goals, integrate, and report/communicate. Not surprisingly, the GRI G4 Sustainability Reporting Guidelines are mentioned specifically in terms of effective reporting and communication (Global Reporting Initiative, United

---

3 There are other major international initiatives to guide companies with regards to the planning, implementation and reporting of initiatives contributing towards the ten principles, the MDGs and related issues. These initiatives include the World Business Council for Sustainable Development (WBCSD) toolkit (the two most explicitly focused on the MDGs being Measuring Impact Framework and Doing Business in the World), the International Finance Corporation's (IFC) Environmental and Social Performance, the Carbon Disclosure Project, the Global Reporting Initiative's G4 Guidelines and the International Integrated Reporting Council's reporting framework. For more information on reporting standards, see www.carrotsandsticks.net.

Nations Global Compact, World Business Council on Sustainable Development, 2015a, p. 27).

Making global standards local

It was mentioned earlier that there is a second tension that corporations have to negotiate: that between global perspective and local application. Global standards have an important, but limited, role to play. The value of universal moral frameworks such as the UN Global Compact or the SDGs is limited, to some extent, by the lack of local specificity. This is a weakness by design and—by implication—not a weakness at all if the limitation is acknowledged. The success of the UN Global Compact measured against its own objectives is the subject of an ongoing debate (Williams, 2004; Williams 2014b) and will not be discussed here.

It has been argued that the ten principles of the UN Global Compact should be viewed as hypernorms in terms of Donaldson and Dunfee's Integrative Social Contracts Theory (Donaldson and Dunfee, 1999), and that the principles, collectively, can be regarded as a hypothetical macro contract (Malan, 2015). For the principles to qualify as hypernorms there are certain conditions that must be met: they should relate to general consensus; be aligned with existing standards; be supported by major stakeholder groups; be consistent with major religions and philosophies; and be consonant with existing legal frameworks. It is clear that all ten UN Global Compact principles are supported by the majority of these types of evidence, although for the sake of this argument one has to exclude the fact that the principles are part of a well-known international standard (the UN Global Compact), since that would constitute a circular argument.

It has further been argued that the way in which hypernorms limit moral free space[4] can provide practical guidance to companies that have subscribed to the UN Global Compact, not only in how they need to adhere to the ten principles, but how they can structure and implement their broader corporate responsibility programmes. The following statement by Donaldson and Dunfee (1999, p. 50) supports this position: "Since such principles [hypernorms] are designed to impose limiting conditions on *all* micro contracts, they cannot be derived from a single micro contract, but must emanate from a source that speaks with univocal authority for all micro contracts".

The same argument applies to the SDGs. Support for the goals themselves is almost intuitive, similar to the high-level support required for the ten UN Global Compact principles. But because the principles themselves are described as a

---

4 Moral free space is defined as "[t]he freedom of individuals to form or join communities and to act jointly to establish moral rules applicable to the members of the community" (Donaldson and Dunfee, 1999, p. 38).

hypothetical contract, the real impact of support can only be articulated through micro contracts. In the South African case, the National Development Plan provides an interesting intermediary to enable localized and relevant action.

The South African National Development Plan

South Africa has made significant progress since the end of Apartheid, but the country still has some major shortcomings in its development path. Since 1994, the country has designed and (partially) implemented different development strategies, including the Reconstruction and Development Programme (RDP), Growth, Employment and Redistribution (GEAR), the Accelerated and Shared Growth Initiative for South Africa (ASGISA) and the New Growth Path (NGP).

The National Planning Committee (NPC) was established by the South African Government in May 2009 to develop the country's Vision 2030. The NPC's Diagnostic Report identified nine main challenges still plaguing the country: 1) Too few people work; 2) The standard of education for most black learners is of poor quality; 3) Infrastructure is poorly located, under-maintained and insufficient to foster higher growth; 4) Spatial patterns exclude the poor from the fruits of development; 5) The economy is overly and unsustainably resources intensive; 6) A widespread disease burden is compounded by a failing public health system; 7) Public services are uneven and often of poor quality; 8) Corruption is widespread; and 9) South Africa remains a divided society.

To overcome these challenges and realize Vision 2030, the NDP was released in August 2012 and identified 12 key focus areas, included in Table 5. The NPC recognized that the plan can only be a success if it is championed by the South African society at large, including the private sector. There is however no clear strategy and call to action to get South African companies to contribute towards addressing the priorities set out in the plan. Table 5 maps the focus areas of the NDP against the SDGs.

Table 5 NDP and SDG comparison

NDP focus areas	Relevant SDGs
An economy that will create more jobs	End poverty in all its forms everywhere (1) Promote sustained, inclusive and sustainable economic growth, full and productive employment and decent work for all (8)
Improving infrastructure	Build resilient infrastructure, promote inclusive and sustainable industrialization and foster innovation (9)
Transition to a low-carbon economy	All the environmental goals (6, 7, 12, 13, 14, 15)

Continued

An inclusive and integrated rural economy	End hunger, achieve food security and improved nutrition and promote sustainable agriculture (2)
Reversing the spatial effects of apartheid	Reduce inequality within and among countries (10)
Improving the quality of education, training and innovation	Ensure inclusive and equitable quality education and promote lifelong learning opportunities for all (4)
Quality health care for all	Ensure healthy lives and promote well-being for all at all ages (3)
Social protection	Achieve gender equality and empower all women and girls (5)
Building safer communities	Make cities and human settlements inclusive, safe, resilient and sustainable (11) Build resilient infrastructure, promote inclusive and sustainable industrialization and foster innovation (9)
Reforming the public services	Promote peaceful and inclusive societies for sustainable development, provide access to justice for all and build effective, accountable and inclusive institutions at all levels (16)
Fighting corruption	Promote peaceful and inclusive societies for sustainable development, provide access to justice for all and build effective, accountable and inclusive institutions at all levels (16)
Transforming society and uniting the country	Promote peaceful and inclusive societies for sustainable development, provide access to justice for all and build effective, accountable and inclusive institutions at all levels (16)

In a project initiated by the World Economic Forum's Global Agenda Council on Values, action items were selected as specific and practical ways in which South African companies can support the National Development Plan. Some of these can be initiated by companies at the individual level (e.g. reduce youth unemployment), while others require partnerships between companies as well as with government and civil society (e.g. the establishment of a fibre-optic network or climate change centre). Table 6 provides proposed action items that were selected for consideration. Similar to SDG 17 (the global partnership), NDP action item 119 (a social compact) is somewhat vague and redundant.

Table 6 Potential action areas for corporations to support the NDP

Focus area	Relevant NDP action item (#)
Economy and employment	Facilitate agreement with unions on entry level wages (7) Reduce youth unemployment (9)
Economic infrastructure	Establish a national, regional and municipal fibre-optic network (29)
Environmental sustainability and resilience	Establish an independent climate change centre (31)
Inclusive rural economy	Activate rural economies through improved infrastructure and service delivery (37)
SA in the region and the world	Focus trade penetration in fast-growing markets: Asia, Brazil, Africa (40)
Transforming human settlements	Develop strategy for densification of cities (43) Invest in safe, reliable and affordable public transport (44) Housing finance—including subsidies and employer housing schemes—that allows for greater household choice, spatial mix and flexibility (46)
Improving education, training and innovation	Nutrition programme for pregnant women and young children; early childhood development and care programme (< 3s) Recognize top-performing schools in the private and public sectors (56) Build strong relationship between college sector and industry (62) Provide comprehensive tertiary bursaries (cost of tuition, books, accommodation and other living expenses) (66)
Health care for all	Promote healthy diets and physical activity (68) Contribute to the prevention and control of epidemic burdens by deterring and treating HIV/AIDS, new epidemics

Continued

Social protection	Identify elements of comprehensive food security and nutrition strategy and launch campaign (76) Create incentives that encourage a culture of individual saving for risks and loss of income due to old age, illness, injury or loss of work for workers (79) Pilot mechanisms and incentives to assist the unemployed to access the labour market (79)
Building safer communities	Participation in community crime prevention and safety initiatives (85) Mobilize youth for inner city safety (87)
Building a capable and developmental state	Use placements and secondments to enable staff to develop experience of working in other spheres of government (96) Develop regional utilities to deliver some local government services on an agency basis (98) Measure to protect the security of whistle-blowers (103) Corruption in the private sector to be reported on and monitored by an agency similar to the Public Protector (107)
Nation building and social cohesion	Prominent display of bill of responsibilities in the work place (111) Campaigns against racism, sexism, homophobia and/or xenophobia (112) Employment Equity to continue and new models of BEE to be explored (114) Incentivize the production and distribution of all art forms that facilitate healing, nation building and dialogue (116) All South Africans to learn at least one indigenous language, business to encourage and reward employees who do so (117) *Work towards a social compact for equity* (119)

The following South African companies are listed as UN Global Compact signatories but have either been delisted because of non-communication or requested removal, or are currently listed as non-communicating:

- ▶ Delisted because of failure to communicate: Aerosud Holdings, Bathabile Holdings, BHP Billiton SA, Bowman Gilfillan, Health Management Institute, Merck, PG Group, Rainbow Farms, Rand Water, The South African Forestry Company

- ▶ Delisted after withdrawal requested: Accenture South Africa and Old Mutual South Africa

- ▶ Currently non-communicating: Coca-Cola Sabco Pty Ltd, FirstRand, South African Airways, South African Express Airways, South African Post Office

The table below summarizes the most recent COPs submitted by active South African signatories of the UN Global Compact. It lists the title of the document that was submitted as the COP (in some cases multiple documents), gives an indication of the length of the document and an indication of the number of references in the respective documents to either the SDGs or the NDP. It should be noted that the draft SDGs were already available in 2014 (Chasek et al., 2014) and it would therefore not be unreasonable to expect some companies to mention the SDGs before the actual launch date in September 2015.

Table 7 Analysis of COPs

Company	Title	Date	Pages	SDG references	NDP references
Afrisam	Sustainability Report	2014	100	0	0
Altron	Communication on Progress Report	2015	28	1	0
Anglogold Ashanti	Annual Sustainable Development Report Summary	2014	44	0	0
Aspen	Communication on Progress Report	2015	4	0	0
Barloworld	Communication on Progress	2015	24	0	0
Deloitte	Global Report	2015	77	0	0
Distell	Sustainability Report	2015	81	0	0
Edcon	Communication on Progress	2016	15	0	0
Eskom	Communication on Progress	2015	56	0	2

Continued

Exxaro	Communication on Progress	2014	14	0	0
Firstrand	Annual Integrated Report	2015	552	0	0
Goldfields (1)	Integrated Annual Report	2014	125	1	0
Goldfields (2)	Communication on Progress 2014 Guidance Sheet	2014	9	0	0
Implats	Sustainable Development Report	2015	152	0	11
Investec	Communication of Progress	2015	8	0	0
Mondi	Communication on Progress	2015	318	0	0
MTN	Communication of Progress	2014	43	0	0
Nedbank	Communication of Progress	2014	69	0	1
Netcare	Active COP	2015	12	1	0
Oceana	Communication on Progress	2015	21	0	0
Public Investment Corporation	Communication on Progress	2016	19	0	1
Pick n Pay	Communication on Progress	2015	5	0	0
Richards Bay	Sustainability Report	2014	72	0	0
Royal Bafokeng	Integrated Report	2014	133	0	0
Sanlam (1)	Strategic Review	2014	8	0	0
Sanlam (2)	Sustainability Report	2014	124	0	1
Sanlam (3)	Annual Report	2014	368	0	1
Sappi	Sustainability Report	2015	151	1	0
Sasol (1)	Annual Integrated Report	2015	106	0	1
Sasol (2)	Sustainable Development Information	2015	58	0	1

Continued

Company	Title	Date	Pages	SDG references	NDP references
Sibanye	Integrated Annual Report	2014	240	0	1
Sun International	Integrated Annual Report	2015	88	0	0
Tongaat Hulett	Communication on Progress	2015	2	0	0
Transnet	Sustainability Report	2015	44	0	4
Unilever	Global Compact Advanced COP Self-Assessment	2015	16	1	0
Woolworths	Good Business Journey Report	2015	55	1	1

The average report length was 100 pages, and in all the reports combined there were only six references to the SDGs by six different companies. There were 25 references to the NDP by ten different companies, with one (Implats) providing 11 references. By itself, the number of references to either the SDGs or NDP does not indicate more or less support for the initiatives. At best, this provides insight into an underlying corporate consciousness of the initiatives themselves. It is perfectly possible for a company not to reference an initiative, yet to behave in a way that is much more closely aligned with the objectives than those of a corporate that has reported extensively. That is the inherent weakness of corporate reporting and is the reason why many stakeholders are sceptical of corporate reports, even those ones that have been assured by external service providers.

In general, the references to both the SDGs and the NDP are fairly generic, as illustrated by the two examples below:

From the Netcare CEO statement (Netcare Ltd, 2015, p. 2):

> We are committed to making the Global Compact and its principles part of the strategy, culture and day-to-day operations of our company, and to engaging in collaborative projects which advance the broader development goals of the United Nations, particularly the Millennium Development Goals which have been replaced by the Sustainable Development Goals.

From the Woolworths report (2015, p. 7): "We have referenced the UN Post-2015 Development Framework and its sustainable development goals in our strategy determination process".

As mentioned above, the only exception—both in terms of the SDGs and the NDP—is provided by Implats (2015), which provides a detailed two-page table to illustrate its support for the NDP (Implats, 2015, pp. 98-99). Examples from this table are provided in Table 8.

Table 8 Implats contributions to NDP

NDP objective	Implats contribution
Transforming the society and uniting the country	Variety of socioeconomic projects, including those mentioned above
An economy that creates more jobs, is more inclusive and that shares the fruits of growth more equitably	Provision of 40,000 direct jobs Procurement spend to suppliers and contractors Enterprise development and training Taxes paid
Building safer communities	Mine crime combating forums
Improving infrastructure	Complementing the accommodation and living conditions initiatives through the provision of schools, clinics and other amenities Mining research and development projects
Reversing the spatial effects of apartheid	Provision of accommodation and improved living conditions for workers
Improving education, training and innovation and providing quality healthcare	Investment in skills development programmes Addressing non-occupational health risks through wellness programmes Community health programmes
Fighting corruption	Zero-tolerance stance on fraud and corruption Provision of whistle-blowing helpline
An inclusive and integral rural economy	Social investment projects (infrastructure, health and housing) Enterprise development initiatives supported local businesses
Transitioning to a low-carbon resource efficient economy	Energy efficiency initiatives, including fuel-cell research Seeking an appropriate policy response to climate change "that does not compromise the competitiveness of our sector"

Source: Implats (2015, pp. 98-99)

It could be argued that many of the activities reported on, for example the extensive information provided by Implats, would have been provided in a different format had the NDP not existed, and can therefore not be listed as "NDP projects". It is also important to perform a close reading of the information provided. The framing of the climate change policy response "that does not compromise the competitiveness of our sector" (Implats, 2015, p. 99) does not really inspire confidence.

Although not empirically verifiable, it is postulated that the low levels of disclosure by South African corporations indicate a lack of engagement with important societal issues. It is anticipated that the SDG Compass will have an impact on the way in which UN Global Compact signatories will report on the SDGs in future.

Conclusion

The challenges faced by the global economy are complex and multi-dimensional. It is therefore to be expected that there will be no easy solutions, and that the contributions that can be made by corporations will not be straightforward either. The SDGs and the UN Global Compact provide global frameworks for corporate initiatives, and national initiatives such as the South African National Development Plan, industry initiatives or corporate activities provide the local application opportunities. In addition, corporations are grappling with questions about the purpose of business—while popular approaches such as CSV are gaining ground, there seems to be a growing realization that there is (or should be, depending on the paradigm) a normative component that should be acknowledged. This component finds expression in global goals such as the SDGs and global initiatives such as the UN Global Compact. Every corporation should be encouraged to embrace these and to become a force for good.

References

Chasek, P., Dafoe, J., Lebada, A.M., & Leone, F. (2014). Summary of the Thirteenth Session of the UN General Assembly Open Working Group on Sustainable Development Goals. *Earth Negotiations Bulletin*, 32(13). Retrieved from: http://www.iisd.ca/vol32/enb3213e.html

Crane, A., Palazzo, G., Spence, L.J., & Matten, D. (2014). Contesting the value of "creating shared value". *California Management Review*, 56(2), 130-153.

Donaldson, T., & Dunfee, T. (1999). *Ties That Bind: A Social Contracts Approach to Business Ethics*. Boston, MA: Harvard University Press.

Francis I (2015). *Encyclical letter "Laudato Si": On Care for Our Common Home*. Vatican City: Vatican Press. Retrieved from: http://w2.vatican.va/content/francesco/en/encyclicals/documents/papa-francesco_20150524_enciclica-laudato-si.html

Friedman, M. (2002). The social responsibility of business is to increase its profits. In T. Donaldson, M. Cording & P. Werhane (Eds.), *Ethical Issues in Business: A Philosophical Approach* (7th ed.), (pp. 33-38). New Jersey: Prentice Hall.

Global Reporting Initiative, UN Global Compact, World Business Council for Sustainable Development (2015). *SDG Compass*. Retrieved from: http://www.sdgcompass.org

Global Reporting Initiative, United Nations Global Compact, World Business Council on Sustainable Development (2015a). *SDG Compass: The Guide for Business Action on the SDGs*. Retrieved from: http://sdgcompass.org/wp-content/uploads/2016/05/019104_SDG_Compass_Guide_2015_v29.pdf

Goodpaster, K., & Matthews, J. (1982). Can a corporation have a conscience? *Harvard Business Review*, 60(1), 132-141.

Implats (2015). *Sustainable Development Report 2015*. Retrieved from: http://www.financialresults.co.za/2015/implat-sd-report-2015/

Kaptein, M., & Wempe, J. (2002). *The Balanced Company: A Theory of Corporate Integrity*. Oxford, UK: Oxford University Press.

Malan, D. (2015). *The Power of Responsibility: Integrative Social Contracts Theory and the United Nations Global Compact*. Unpublished PhD dissertation. University of Stellenbosch.

National Planning Commission (2012). *National Development Plan 2030: Our Future— Make it Work*. Government of South Africa. Retrieved from: http://www.gov.za/issues/national-development-plan-2030

Netcare Ltd. (2015). *UN Global Compact Active COP 2015*. Retrieved from: https://www.unglobalcompact.org/participation/report/cop/create-and-submit/active/194861

Porter, M., & Kramer, M. (2011). Creating shared value. *Harvard Business Review*, Issue HBR Reprint R1101C, 1-17.

Porter, M., & Kramer, M. (2014). A response to Andrew Crane et al's article by Michael E. Porter and Mark R. Kramer. *California Business Review*, 56(2), 149-151.

Smurthwaite, M. (2008). The purpose of the corporation. In O. Williams (Ed.), *Peace through Commerce: Responsible Corporate Citizenship and the Ideals of the United Nations Global Compact* (pp. 13-55). Notre Dame, IN: Notre Dame University Press.

United Nations (1999). Secretary-General proposes global compact on human rights, labour, environment, in address to World Economic Forum in Davos. *UN Press Release SG/SM/6881*. Retrieved from: http://www.un.org/press/en/1999/19990201.sgsm6881.html

United Nations (2000). *United Nations Millennium Declaration*. Retrieved from: http://www.unmillenniumproject.org/documents/ares552e.pdf

United Nations (2015). *Transforming Our World: The 2030 Agenda for Sustainable Development*. Retrieved from: http://www.un.org/ga/search/view_doc.asp?symbol=A/RES/70/1&Lang=E

United Nations (2016). *About Partnerships for SDGs Online Platform*. Retrieved from: https://sustainabledevelopment.un.org/partnerships/about

United Nations Global Compact (2013). *About the UN Global Compact*. Retrieved from: http://www.unglobalcompact.org/AboutTheGC/index.html

United Nations Global Compact (2016). *About the UN Global Compact*. Retrieved from: https://www.unglobalcompact.org/about/faq

Waddock, S. (2013). The future is here for the new CSR: Corporate responsibility and sustainability. In M. Zollo & R. Mele, (Eds.), *The Shared Value Debate: Academic Visions on Corporate Sustainability* (pp. 37-46). Milan: Egea.

Williams, O.F. (2004). The UN Global Compact: The challenge and the promise. *Business Ethics Quarterly*, 14(4), 755-774.

Williams, O.F. (2014a). *Corporate Social Responsibility: The Role of Business in Sustainable Development*. New York: Routledge.

Williams, O.F. (2014b). The United Nations Global Compact: What did it promise? *Journal of Business Ethics,* 122(2), 241-251.

Woolworths Holdings Limited (2015). *2015 Good Business Journey Report.* Retrieved from: http://www.woolworthsholdings.co.za/investor/annual_reports/ar2015/whl_2015_gbj. pdf

Zollo, M., & Mele, R. (Eds.) (2013). *The Shared Value Debate: Academic Visions on Corporate Sustainability.* Milan: Egea.

DOI: [10.9774/GLEAF.4700.2016.de.00012]

Commitments and Appeals to Make a Better World

The Global Compact, Laudato Si and Our Future

James P. Walsh
University of Michigan, USA

Angelo M. Solarino
University of Leeds, UK

We live in a world of need. Business, as perhaps the most powerful transnational force in the world today, can either aggravate or attenuate that need. Recognizing such power, the United Nations launched the Global Compact in 2000 in an effort to change the way firms do business. The UN wants to ensure that a firm is as committed to those it touches with its many activities as it is to its bottom line. Pope Francis entered this world of aspiration in 2015 with his encyclical, Laudato Si. Calling out the failings of a "might is right" world view, he worried that too many of the world's powerful people have lost sight of their humanity. He begged us all to steer clear of the sin of indifference and to work for the common good. Taking stock of these efforts, we conclude that the dynamics of compassion fade and compassion fatigue can undermine our high aspirations. In the end, we propose a complementary initiative that just might serve as an antidote to indifference and help to make the world a better place.

- United Nations Global Compact
- Laudato Si
- Corporate social responsibility
- Compassion fade
- Compassion fatigue

James P. Walsh is a long-time professor at the University of Michigan's Ross School of Business. His research explores the purpose, accountability and control of the firm and even more generally, business itself, in society. Engaging his students with these kinds of questions, he does his best to prepare the next generation to lead in and for society. Jim served as the 65th President of the Academy of Management and the 15th Dean of its Fellows Group. See http://jamespwalsh.com/ for a more comprehensive look at his commitments.

jpwalsh@umich.edu

Angelo M. Solarino is assistant professor at the University of Leeds Business School. His research focuses on questions of corporate governance. Interested in better understanding just who serves on boards of directors and how they make their decisions, he is very curious to learn more about how corporate social responsibility initiatives commingle with firms' other business decisions. Angelo works to foster his students' ethical decision-making with students all over around the world.

a.m.Solarino@leeds.ac.uk

"The world cries out for repair". Margolis and Walsh (2003, p. 268) began their paper entitled "Misery Loves Companies" with these words more than a dozen years ago. Looking at worldwide poverty, public health and education statistics, they painted a picture of a world in need. Observing that corporate wealth and capability mark them as targets for appeal, they took stock of the possibility that corporate social responsibility investments might make the world a better place. While we have seen some progress (United Nations, 2015), the world still cries out for repair and, yes, many in the world still hold out hope that business can make the world a better place.

As the United Nations' 15-year commitment to its Millennium Development Goals (2000–2015) gives way to a new set of aspirations (the Sustainable Development Goals), we learn than 836 million people still live in extreme poverty, that women earn 24% less than men globally, that one in seven children in the world are underweight and one in ten primary school-aged children do not attend school, that 2.1 million people each year are diagnosed with HIV, and that many species of animal life are dying out, marine fish stocks are plummeting, forests are disappearing, and carbon dioxide levels in the atmosphere are increasing (United Nations, 2015). Debate about the role that business may play in both the creation and amelioration of these problems is complex and sometimes contentious. On the one hand, Porter and Stern (2015) tell us that there is a strong correlation between economic growth (GDP per capita) and social progress (assessing the foundations of well-being, opportunity and the provision of basic human needs) in 133 countries. Business activity may make the world a better place. On the other hand, business can also dominate, exploit and degrade the lives of its many stakeholders (Adler et al., 2007). Pope Francis (2015) levelled this charge as succinctly as anyone:

> ... economic powers continue to justify the current global system where priority tends to be given to speculation and the pursuit of financial gain, which fail to take the context into account, let alone the effects on human dignity and the natural environment (Laudato Si, 56).

The challenge then is to beware this contradiction and work to ensure that we get the best from business while mitigating its worst excesses. Enter the United Nations Global Compact and Pope Francis's encyclical letter, Laudato Si.[1]

---

1 The Millennium Development Goals (MDG) were formally adopted by the United Nations on 18 September 2000. Eight goals, brought to life with 21 targets and appraised by 60 indicators marked the world's aspirations. The eight goals were to: (1) eradicate extreme poverty and hunger; (2) achieve universal primary education; (3) promote gender equality and empower women; (4) reduce child mortality; (5) improve maternal health; (6) combat HIV/AIDS, malaria and other diseases; (7) ensure environmental sustainability; and (8) develop a global partnership for development. Fifteen years later, Ban Ki-moon, the Secretary-General of the United Nations declared, "The global mobilization behind the Millennium Development Goals has produced the most successful anti-poverty movement in history". The MGD aspirations can be found at http://www.un.org/sustainabledevelopment/sustainable-development-goals/; the 2015 report, with Ban Ki-moon's

The Global Compact and Laudato Si

Launched in 2000, the United Nations Global Compact is an ambitious effort to change the way firms do business. Grounded in the belief that a corporation's values guide its strategy and operations, the United Nations has worked tirelessly over the past 16 years to ensure that those values reflect a commitment not just to a firm's bottom line but also to those it touches with its many activities. Inspired by the Universal Declaration of Human Rights, the International Labour Organization's Declaration on Fundamental Principles and Rights at Work, the Rio Declaration on Environment and Development, and the United Nations Convention Against Corruption, it asks its member organizations to stand by ten principles as they do their business (principles that speak to human rights, labour, environment and anti-corruption). To join the Global Compact, firms' CEOs must attest not only to their companies' commitments to these principles but also with an annual "Communication on Progress", to share their efforts, and the results of those efforts, to make a better world.[2] Entering a community of like-minded peers, they are encouraged to gather regularly in one of the many Global Compact Local Networks around the world to compare experiences and inspire each other with their commitments. Box 1 captures these ten fundamental principles. Reflecting an interest in the programme, if not necessarily a sustained interest, Figure 1 profiles the cumulative growth in the number of companies that affirmed these principles since the programme's inception (it does not account for those that dropped out).[3] The effort appears to be as successful as it is ambitious.

words, can be found at http://www.un.org/millenniumgoals/2015_MDG_Report/pdf/MDG%202015%20rev%20(July%201).pdf.

Many successes notwithstanding, the United Nations recognized in 2015 that there was still work to be done. And so, on 25 September 2015, the UN voted to work towards achieving a new set of 17 Sustainable Development Goals (SDG). One hundred sixty-nine targets, each tracked by approximately two indicators (the indicators are still being finalized) would help to ensure success. The UN's own words best articulated their aspirations, "We resolve, between now and 2030, to end poverty and hunger everywhere; to combat inequalities within and among countries; to build peaceful, just and inclusive societies; to protect human rights and promote gender equality and the empowerment of women and girls; and to ensure the lasting protection of the planet and its natural resources. We resolve also to create conditions for sustainable, inclusive and sustained economic growth, shared prosperity and decent work for all, taking into account different levels of national development and capacities" (Retrieved from: https://sustainabledevelopment.un.org/post2015/transformingourworld). As laudatory and noteworthy as these international aspirations and commitments are, we are particularly interested in business and its role in making a better world. And so, while aware of the MDG and SDG initiatives and the fact that business can play a role in their realization, we will focus on the UN's direct work with business entities here—the Global Compact.

2 See https://www.unglobalcompact.org/participation/report for a discussion of the reporting requirements and the opportunity to browse the over 28,000 Communication Progress reports submitted to date.

3 We would like to formally thank Ana Blanco and Georg Kell for providing access to their Global Compact data. All of the data pictured in Figures 1–4 come from their files.

Box 1 Ten principles of the United Nations Global Compact

Human rights

Principle 1: Businesses should support and respect the protection of internationally proclaimed human rights; and

Principle 2: make sure that they are not complicit in human rights abuses.

Labour

Principle 3: Businesses should uphold the freedom of association and the effective recognition of the right to collective bargaining;

Principle 4: the elimination of all forms of forced and compulsory labour;

Principle 5: the effective abolition of child labour; and

Principle 6: the elimination of discrimination in respect of employment and occupation.

Environment

Principle 7: Businesses should support a precautionary approach to environmental challenges;

Principle 8: undertake initiatives to promote greater environmental responsibility; and

Principle 9: encourage the development and diffusion of environmentally friendly technologies.

Anti-corruption

Principle 10: Businesses should work against corruption in all its forms, including extortion and bribery.

Figure 1 Cumulative Global Compact signatories, 2000–2015

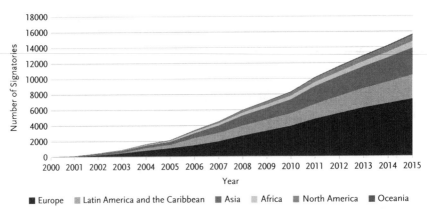

Pope Francis entered this world of aspiration in 2015. His encyclical, Laudato Si (or "On Care for Our Common Home"), can be read as a full-throated rebuke of how we live today. As we see from his quote above, he does not mince words. Asserting that "never have we so hurt and mistreated our common home as we have in the last two hundred years" (LS, 53), he goes on to say that "the earth, our home, is beginning to look more and more like an immense pile of filth" (LS, 21).[4] He concluded, "the post-industrial period may well be remembered as one of the most irresponsible in history" (LS, 165). The good news is that he did more than name a problem; he tried to diagnosis its origins and in that light, offer solutions.

Animated by the same kinds of aspirations that fuel the Global Compact, he is interested in the role that the powerful play in our lives. Concerned about what he calls a "might is right" world view (LS, 82), he worries that too many of the world's most powerful people may have lost sight of their humanity. He writes that such a vision

> ... has engendered immense inequality, injustice and acts of violence against the majority of humanity, since resources end up in the hands of the first comer or the most powerful: the winner takes all. Completely at odds with this model are the ideals of harmony, justice, fraternity and peace as proposed by Jesus (LS, 82).

Foreshadowing his ideas about how to correct course, he argues that "once we lose our humility, and become enthralled with the possibility of limitless mastery over everything, we inevitably end up harming society and the environment" (LS, 224). He believes that our problems can be solved if we "hear both the cry of the earth and the cry of the poor" (LS, 49). Pope Francis wants to "enlighten those who possess power and money that they may avoid the sin of indifference, that they may love the common good, advance the weak, and care for this world in which we live" (LS, 246). His solutions range from a call for "a true world political authority" (LS, 175) that would promote good governance (i.e. "more rigorous regulations, procedures and controls" [LS, 179]) to encouraging the world's citizens to lead more balanced lifestyles (LS, 225), lives marked by contemplative rest (LS, 237) and the ability to discover God in all things (LS, 233). He asks business people to "reject a magical conception of the market" (LS, 190) when considering investments and always to ask if a "proposed activity will not cause serious harm to the environment or to those who inhabit it" (LS, 186). Well aware that people might be inclined to reject his ideas as "romantic illusions or an obstacle to be circumvented" (LS, 54) he notes that "nobody is suggesting a return to the Stone Age, but we do need to slow down and look at reality in a different way" (LS, 114). There is some evidence to suggest that his fear of rejection was unfounded. People listened.

As Pope Francis was one of the world's most admired people at the time of the encyclical's release (18 June 2015), it is no surprise to learn that news of its publication was covered worldwide.[5] Indeed, Factiva counted 629 media

---

4 Note that the convention in a Papal document is to reference the numbered paragraph that houses a quotation, and not a page number.

5 See https://yougov.co.uk/news/2015/01/30/most-admired-2015/ for a list of the world's most admired people in 2015.

mentions by the end of June.[6] A recent look at Google Scholar reveals that his words have already been cited more than 150 times. Just like his colleagues at the United Nations, it may well be that the Pope succeeded in fostering a conversation about values; he may have even changed some people's values for humanity's benefit.

Give their commonality of purpose, it is no surprise to learn that the United Nations asked the Pope to work with them (in an open letter dated 7 August 2015):

> Thus, upon visiting the United Nations in September, we humbly entreat Your Holiness to call directly upon business and financial markets to do more to care for our climate and our common home. We offer our support in convening further dialogue with the UN Global Compact's diverse international network of business actors, civil society partners and labour organisations. In markets all over the world, we want to ensure that the encyclical is heard and the ethic of care it heralds is appreciated (Kell *et al.*, 2015).

Finding no evidence that the Vatican and the United Nations partnered in the way that the letter's authors envisioned, the Vatican did, however, publicly acknowledge the receipt of the letter (Pontifical Council for Justice and Peace, 2015, August 13). And while the Pope did not make much mention of the role of business and financial markets in his speech to the UN General Assembly the next month (on 25 September), he did say,

> The baneful consequences of an irresponsible mismanagement of the global economy, guided only by ambition for wealth and power, must serve as a summons to a forthright reflection on man,

concluding ...

> the defense of the environment and the fight against exclusion demand that we recognize a moral law written into human nature itself.

Very consistent with his call for humility in Laudato Si, he asserted that we must answer to someone or something beyond ourselves.

While Pope Francis appeals to the better nature of our angels, the United Nations offers organizations a path to make the world a better place. Working side-by-side if not hand-in-hand, the missions of the UN and the Vatican are clearly aligned. One might think that an effort led by a religion that counts more than 1.2 billion members and a government organization that speaks for nearly 200 countries is a grand success. Indeed, absent assessment, one can easily imagine that the world is now in very good hands. To paraphrase Pope Francis, we might believe that we are now free of the sin of indifference, that we now love the common good, advance the weak, and care for this world in which

---

6 Quoting from ProQuest's webpage, we learn that "Factiva.com, from Dow Jones, combines over 36,000 sources to give students, faculty, and librarians access to premium content from 200 countries, in 28 languages. Users have access to a wide range of information from newspapers, newswires, industry publications, websites, company reports, and more". See http://proquest.libguides.com/factiva

we live. Our goal here is to investigate this kind of inference. Unfortunately, taking a closer look at the reception of both the Global Compact and Laudato Si, we conclude that we may need to redouble our efforts to realize the dream embedded in these works. We will close by offering a new idea that might well complement these two initiatives.

Indifference?

While it is difficult to tell if anyone's heart or mind has been touched by these efforts, we can certainly track the level of interest in this work. Let's first consider the Global Compact. Figure 1 shows strong positive growth in interest over the first 15 years of its existence. While that may be true, Figure 1 does not account for membership churn. Figure 2 pictures the dynamics of this membership. As we can see, the membership has been anything but stable, particularly since 2010. While to be sure the Global Compact has attracted new members over the years, it has also borne witness to quite a number of departures; 1,010, 1,395, 1,227, 551, 920 and 1,407 companies left the Global Compact in the years 2010 through 2015, respectively. While 15,641 companies have signed on to the Global Compact since 2000, 7,518 (or 48% of them) did not sustain their commitment. While to be sure, the number of active signatories to the Global Compact continues to grow, Figure 2 shows us that this growth appears to be levelling off. This is hardly an unalloyed success story.

Figure 2 Dynamics of Global Compact membership, 2000–2015

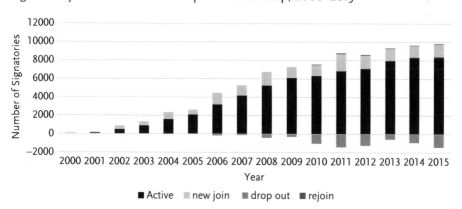

In addition, membership is not evenly distributed around the world. Janney *et al.* (2009) might have predicted as much. They looked at the market reaction to 175 multinational corporations' (MNCs) decisions to join the Global Compact.[7]

---

7 As is true of all empirical studies, we need to be alert to the quality of the evidence. The authors were careful to note how they compiled their data. As of December 2006, the

They found that the 82 headquartered in Europe enjoyed a positive two-day (-1,0) cumulative annual return of 2.019%, while the 23 headquartered in the USA suffered a two-day loss of 1.769%. They attributed the effect to the firms' very different political, cultural and economic environments. Europe appears to provide a much more hospitable environment for firms to join the Global Compact than does the USA. Figure 3 depicts annual membership growth in six regions of the world: Europe, Latin America and the Caribbean, Asia, Africa, Northern America, and Oceania. Europe and the Latin America and the Caribbean region capture the lion's share of signatories. The Europe/North America difference jumps right out at us. Few North American companies appear eager to abide by these ten principles. Taking a closer look at country by country membership, Figure 4(b) pictures the top 20 signatories in 2015. With Europe accounting for nearly half of the signatories that year (Figure 4a), we see that Spain and France lead the way. Nearly a quarter of all of the Global Compact's members come from two countries that comprise just 1.5% of the world's population.[8]

Figure 3 Geography of Global Compact membership

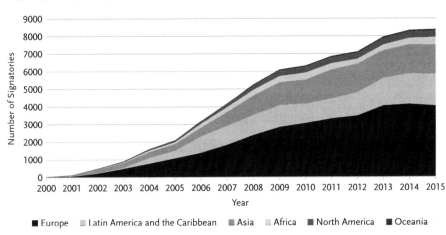

authors found 3,457 organizations to be affiliated with the Global Compact: 1,432 were for-profit firms; 379 of them were publicly traded; and 175 of them were multinational corporations where the Global Compact announcement decisions were not confounded with other information announcements. Of course, we await an investigation of the market reactions to MNC affiliation decisions made in the past ten years. For those new to event study methodology, Brown and Warner (1985) provide a succinct introduction to this work.

8 Compare the 2015 populations of Spain and France (46,121,699 and 64,395,345, respectively) with the population of the world that year (7,349,472,099). These data were retrieved from the Worldometers database. Spain's population data, for example, can be found here: http://www.worldometers.info/world-population/spain-population/

Figure 4 A closer look at the geography of Global Compact membership, 2015; (a) by percentage and (b) by most represented countries

(a)

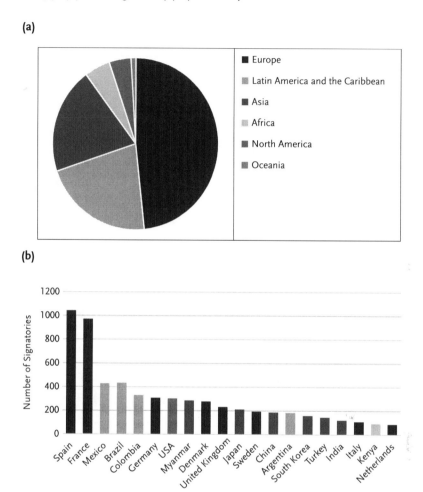

(b)

Public interest in the Global Compact is waning. Two kinds of data point to that conclusion. First, media interest in the Global Compact is weakening, if not diminishing. Figure 5 captures and combines two kinds of data from Factiva. Distinguishing between what might be called "internal", self-generated press release coverage and "external", media-generated coverage, we see that while firms are not shy about touting their commitments to the Global Compact, media interest is flagging. Figure 6 gives us a scaled look at the general public's interest in the Global Compact. Looking at worldwide web search activity for the phrase "United Nations Global Compact" and the shorter search term "Global Compact", we see an unmistakable downward trend in the public's interest in this initiative.[9]

---

9 Asking Google for their raw data (i.e. the actual number of searches each year), they politely declined to share it with us. They explained, "the reason being that Google's earnings are tied to search volume, and therefore the raw info can't be shared externally".

Figure 5 Global Compact media mentions
Source: Factiva

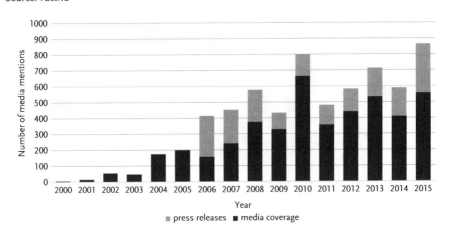

Year

■ press releases ■ media coverage

Figure 6 Global Compact Google web search activity, 2004–2015
Source: Google Trends

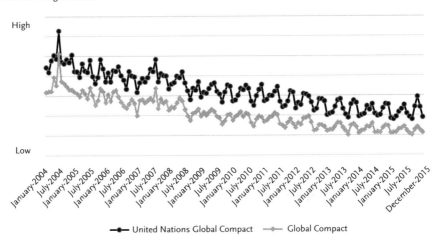

—●— United Nations Global Compact   —◆— Global Compact

Notwithstanding the initial flurry of interest in Laudato Si, it appears that interest in this document has also waned. Looking again at Factiva, Figure 7 pictures the burst of media attention that accompanied its June publication but with the exception of some attention that autumn, likely attendant to the Pope's visit to America (from 22 to 27 September), current interest is negligible (we see only 37 media mentions in June 2016). A look at worldwide Google web search data paints a similar picture. Looking at Google Trend analyses (just as we did in Figure 6), Figure 8 reveals a good deal of public interest upon its release and again, likely attendant to his visit to the USA. We see minimal interest afterwards.

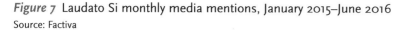

Figure 7 Laudato Si monthly media mentions, January 2015–June 2016

Source: Factiva

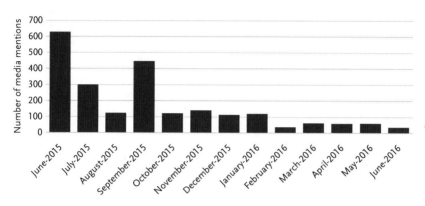

Figure 8 Laudato Si Google web search activity, January 2015–June 2016

Source: Google Trends

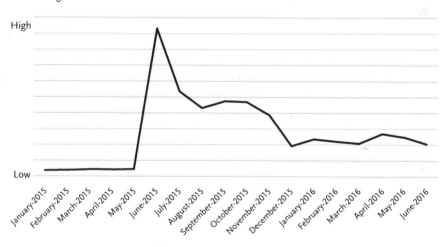

All in all, the information reviewed in Figures 2–8 suggests that we, powerful and powerless alike, may have a hard time avoiding the sin of indifference. To be sure, some companies and some people do care, but on balance we do not see much sustained interest in these aspirations for our shared humanity. Consider the fact that 15,641 companies thought enough of the Global Compact's ten principles to publicly affirm them. Holding aside the fact that nearly half of them could not sustain their commitment, what does this level of interest tell us? Absent a denominator, we really do not know. The good news is that Dun and Bradstreet (2015) give us some sense of the magnitude of business activity worldwide. It turns out that they have data in hand on 134,968,036 companies (from 235 countries). Divide 15,641 by 134,968,036 and we learn that only one hundredth of 1% of the companies in the world can stand behind these principles … even if only for a year.

And whither Laudato Si? Like all papal encyclicals, it will live "forever". It is now a part of the magisterium of the Catholic Church. Beyond that, the Vatican took the occasion of the first anniversary of its publication to create a webpage dedicated to keeping its hope alive.[10] The webpage is home to all kind of news, writing, interviews, conference and seminar announcements (and synopses of the gatherings), and more. To be sure, Catholic dioceses, parishes, schools and environmental groups also work to keep the Pope's words alive in their own unique ways. The Church certainly stands behind its words. But of course, needing to attend to the spiritual lives of over 1 billion people, it does other work too. For example, Pope Francis (2016) recently turned his attention to the life of the family in his apostolic exhortation entitled "Amoris Laetitia" (or "The Joy of Love"). This is a meditation on the well-being of the family in contemporary society. In the end, no one lives our lives for us. It is up to us, the citizens of the world, to listen and just maybe heed the call of the leaders and prophets in our midst to make the world a better place. What is the likelihood that we will overcome our indifference and act? The evidence we presented here gives some cause for concern. There are limits to compassion. We may need to overcome a mix of compassion fatigue and compassion fade if we are to stand a chance.

Compassion's limits

There are two different but related reasons why people may be inclined to meet misery with indifference. One speaks to our inability to grasp problems as they unfold on a grand scale (i.e. compassion fade). Meet an impoverished individual face-to-face and we are filled with empathy and sympathy; hear that nearly a billion people live in extreme poverty, however, and we are impassive. We simply cannot fathom what it means for a billion people to suffer. Suffering on such a grand scale becomes an abstraction that, paradoxically, leaves us unmoved. We cannot connect. That said, we do sometimes act for the common good. The problem is that after a time the quest can overwhelm us; we then retreat to a world of self-interest (i.e. compassion fatigue). If we are to move forward in service of our shared humanity, we will need to understand and address both sources of inaction.

Compassion fade

Joseph Stalin is purported to have said, "The death of one man is a tragedy, the death of millions is a statistic". Speaking to this same phenomenon, Mother Teresa said, "If I look at the mass, I will never act. If I look at the one, I will". Trying to understand why and how people are able to sit back and watch one

---

10 http://www.laudatosi.va/content/giustiziaepace/en.html

genocide after another, Slovic (2007, p. 80) called these kinds of insights "a powerful and deeply unsettling insight into human nature".[11] He went on to frame our problem:

> Most people are caring and will exert great effort to rescue "the one" whose needy plight comes to their attention. These same good people, however, often become numbly indifferent to the plight of "the one" who is "one of many" in a much greater problem. Why does this occur?

If the world can stand by and watch 800,000 men, women and children die in just 100 days at the hands of their fellow citizens (in Rwanda's 1994 genocide), then what hope is there to mobilize action against a world of extreme poverty, malnutrition and illness or one marked by the exploitation of the environment and others for profit? Our hope lies in unearthing the mechanism of indifference. It turns out that affect matters. As Stalin knew, statistics are bereft of emotion. People are unmoved by an abstract, analytic and rational picture, no matter how desperate the scene. Indeed, Slovic (2007, p. 83) pointed out that a motivation to act is rooted in "feelings such as empathy, sympathy, compassion, sadness, pity, and distress". Our challenge then is to "impart the feelings that are needed for rational action" (Slovic, 2007, p. 86). We will offer an idea to address that challenge but before we do, we need to recognize that "our capacity to feel is limited" (Slovic and Västfjäll, 2015, p. 33). Even if motivated to act, there is no guarantee that the actors will see their commitments through.

Compassion fatigue

We know that care givers, first responders, military personnel, judges and others that come face-to-face with victims and perpetrators of trauma can become overwhelmed by the emotional burden of facing misery day in and day out. Figley (1995) noted that such people suffer a kind of "secondary trauma" and disengage, calling the phenomenon "compassion fatigue". It is in this sense that Slovic and Västfjäll (2015) remind us that even when reformers have the world's attention, they may not have it for long. Shifting levels of analysis from an individual to a nation, Schlesinger (1986) observed cycles in history, cycles that oscillate between a commitment to public purpose and a commitment to a private self-interest. A commitment to a purpose greater than the self in time yields to a life of self-absorption, which in due time will yield again to a life marked by a commitment to public purpose, that will yet again give way to a life of self-interest. This kind of oscillation may reflect the fact that we humans are one of only a very few species on earth that commingle a capacity for cooperation with a more typical competitive

---

11 Observing the murders in Armenia (1915), Ukraine (1932–1933), Nazi Germany/Holocaust (WWII), Bangladesh (1971), Cambodia (1975–1979), the former Yugoslavia (1990s), Rwanda (1994), Zimbabwe (2000), and most recently, in the Congo and Darfur, Slovic (2007, p. 81) called this "A Century of Genocide".

drive for self-interest (Wilson, 2014). Both other-serving and self-serving inclinations are baked into the nature of our species. Schlesinger Jr (1986) does not look for the origins of the cycle in biology but he does situate it in the kind of human nature that caught Paul Slovic's eye. Schlesinger Jr (1986) talks about how each cycle breeds its own contradictions. His words below capture the essence of his argument. The first excerpt speaks to how public purpose will yield to self-interest and the second speaks to how self-interest will yield to public purpose.

> Public action, in its effort to better our condition, piles up a lot of change in rather short order ... Sustained public action, moreover, is emotionally exhausting. A nation's capacity for high tension political commitment is limited. Nature insists on a respite. People can no longer gird themselves for heroic effort. They yearn to immerse themselves in the privacies of life (p. 28).

> Epochs of private interest breed contradictions too ... Segments of the population fall behind in the acquisitive race. Intellectuals are estranged. Problems neglected become acute, threaten to become unmanageable and demand remedy. People grow bored with selfish motives and vistas, weary of materialism as the ultimate goal ... They are ready for a trumpet to sound (pp. 28-29).

While Schlesinger Jr (1986) builds on his father's work, work that traces this public purpose/private interest cycle back to 1765 (Schlesinger, 1949), we recognize that people today are more familiar with 20th-century US history than they are with its 18th- and 19th-century history.[12] As such, we will just picture the general ebb and flow of these forces through the 20th century and to the present day. Beginning with Theodore Roosevelt's presidency in 1901 and ending with an observation about Donald Trump's presidential bid, we hope that Table 1 provides enough detail to illustrate the cycle. The point here is that we may be at the end of a public purpose cycle.[13] Indeed, the waning interest in the Global Compact and the passing attention to Laudato Si may say as much. Any effort to address the world's problems today will confront the timeless problem of compassion fade and just maybe a brewing inclination to turn inward. What to do?

---

12 Schlesinger (1949, pp. 77-92) noted eight periods, four liberal and four conservative (in his words), between 1765 and 1901. They begin with the Stamp Act of 1765 and the colonists' resistance to English imperialism (liberal) and end with Grant's election in 1869, one that ushered in a long period of unfettered business enterprise (conservative): 1765–1787, 1787–1801, 1801–1816, 1816–1829, 1829–1841, 1841–1861, 1861–1869, 1869–1901.

13 Of course, this just speaks to the cycle in the United States. We have no idea if countries operate on their own cycles or perhaps with the force of globalization, the cycles align worldwide (or to be fair, we do not even know if such cycles are universal). That said, some see the June 2016 "Brexit" vote in the UK as foreshadowing a Trump presidency (Kay, 2016). Perhaps the citizens of the UK and the US are beginning to suffer compassion fatigue these days. (Reviewing the page proofs on 22 November 2016, we see that Katty Kay was prescient.)

Table 1 Cycles of American history

1901–1919	Progressivism, Square Deal, WWI	Public purpose	Theodore Roosevelt's Square Deal focused on the conservation of natural resources, control of corporations and consumer protection. Woodrow Wilson led a war effort and peace process that galvanized the nation.
1919–1931	Roaring 20s, Jazz Age	Private interest	Warren G. Harding reduced taxes on the wealthy (taxes levied to fund the war), encouraged the Securities and Exchange Commission, Interstate Commerce Commission and Justice Department to cooperate with corporations, and limited immigration. Calvin Coolidge also supported the private sector. Notably, he once remarked, "the chief business of the American people is business".
1931–1947	Depression, New Deal, WWII	Public purpose	Franklin Roosevelt's response to the Great Depression focused on the "3 Rs" (Relief, Recovery and Reform): relief for the unemployed and poor; recovery of the economy; and reform of the financial system to prevent a repeat depression. Fighting both the Depression and the Axis powers united the nation in compelling collective purposes.
1947–1961	Post-war recovery, baby boom, suburban growth, prosperity	Private interest	The GI Bill of Rights enabled soldiers to educate themselves and purchase homes. Emerging as a global power, the US's post-war economy blossomed. Heavy investments in public infrastructure provided jobs and a foundation for economic prosperity.
1961–1977	New Frontier, Great Society, Civil rights, Women's rights, Viet Nam war, Watergate	Public purpose	John F. Kennedy's election signalled a new era of activism. His New Frontier, Lyndon B. Johnson's Great Society programmes, and even many of Richard Nixon's policies were aspirational. A focus on poverty alleviation, civil rights, women's rights, labour protection, the environment, government accountability and both fighting and protesting the Viet Nam war consumed the nation.

Continued

1977–2001	Carter's malaise speech, Reaganomics, Clinton's welfare to work reform	Private interest	Jimmy Carter chastised Americans for turning inward, arguing that "too many of us now tend to worship self-indulgence and consumption". Ronald Reagan advocated tax reductions to spur economic growth, control of the money supply to curb inflation, economic deregulation, and reduction in government spending. Bill Clinton focused on streamlining government and limiting welfare programmes. Christopher Lasch's book, *The Culture of Narcissism* and the movie *Wall Street* (popularizing the saying, "Greed is good") were cultural touchstones.
2001–2016	September 11th, two wars, Obamacare, gay marriage, business as an agent of world benefit	Public purpose	The 9/11 attack united the nation and prompted wars in Iraq and Afghanistan. George W. Bush expanded Medicare, focused on education (No Child Left Behind Act) and invested heavily in the international fight against HIV/AIDS. Barack Obama will be known for reforming heathcare and supporting LGBTQ rights (gay marriage was legalized nationwide). The Global Compact is just one of many initiatives that reflect a growing awareness that business can be an agent of world benefit.
2016–?		Private interest	The rise of Donald Trump with his anti-immigrant, isolationist ideas may signal a move away from public purpose and towards private interest.

A new idea

While the world cries out for repair, the psychology of compassion fade and fatigue works against sweeping efforts to better the world. As difficult as it may be to address fade, it may be tougher still to inspire a world caught in compassion fatigue. Timing matters. Having said that, we cannot tell the world's impoverished, malnourished, uneducated and sick to wait a generation for the rest of the world to act. And so, we would like to offer an idea to address the compassion fade and in so doing, just maybe convince those who can help to help.

Recall that Paul Slovic (2007, p. 86) identified our challenge—we need to find a way to "impart the feelings that are needed for rational action". Slovic and Slovic (2015) answered the challenge eight years later. They ended their book with these words:

> ... one of the essential lessons of our book is that *how* information is communicated (whether in large quantities or small)—such as the intertwining of numerical and narrative descriptions or sometimes the extension of abstract numerical data into narrative or visual analogues—may be particularly essential to our apprehending (and perhaps counteracting) the dangers and injustices human beings impose upon ourselves and the planet (p. 220).

We need to find a way to use narrative and visual information to bring the lives of those in need to life. Indeed, vivid depictions might stimulate public-spirited action even as the cycle of history spins towards self-interest. As business professors, our eyes turn to the business community, to those who can remediate their own harmful behaviour and to those who can use their capacities to solve the world's pressing problems (see Kania and Kramer, 2011; Porter and Kramer, 2011; Reiser, 2011; London, 2016). In the end, no one lives our lives for us. It is up to us, the citizens of the world, to listen and just maybe heed the call of the leaders and prophets in our midst to make the world a better place.

Consider coffee. Ponte (2002) pictured the value chain that links coffee drinkers the world over with farmers in places like Africa, Asia and South America (not to mention all of the intermediaries who work to turn coffee beans into the beverage so many drink every morning). This is a lucrative industry. With 57% of the US population being coffee drinkers, the US retail coffee market generated $35.7 billion in revenues and a $1.9 billion profit in 2015 (Turk, 2015). To be sure, we know that this kind of wealth is not equally shared across the value chain. For example, retailers make much more money than farmers (Valkila *et al.*, 2010). No one is saying that everyone must share the wealth equally. Still, if we could only see that our lives—rich and poor alike—are intimately connected as we produce, sell and consume our goods and services, then the well-off among us just might be moved with compassion to address the problems of the less fortunate we touch with our value chains every day. The challenge is to bring those lives to light.

We are inspired by Smolan and Cohen's (1986) effort 30 years ago to reveal the fullness of life in America. Recall that they dispersed 200 photographers all over the country on 2 May 1986 to chronicle that day in American history. The results were published in a compelling coffee table book. A grand success, they followed up (alone and together) to picture life in over a dozen other states, countries and continents. Twelve years later, Bamberger and Davidson (1998) captured the closing of an American factory in a very compelling fashion. A photographer (Bamberger) and an English professor (Davidson), they joined forces to capture the events in image and word. While we may know the economic reasons for offshoring (Blinder, 2006; Blinder and Krueger, 2013), for example, takes a project like this to bring the human experience of dislocation to life. Inspired by these past efforts, we imagine a project where we picture and reveal the humanity in our world's value chains.

Figure 9 captures the kind of image we might see on the cover of a book and documentary film; in this case, one that would bring to life everyone responsible for our morning coffee. The idea is to map the complete value chain and then photograph, film and interview the people who work at each stop along the way. Sitting down with a cup of coffee to leaf through the book or watch the documentary, the coffee consumer would meet everyone who put that cup of coffee in his or her hand: the famers, roasters, exporters, traders, wholesalers and retailers, not to mention the back office staff that enable these people to do their work, as well as all those who transport the coffee around the world and, yes, the politicians, bankers and insurance professionals that enable the industry to function. Working with both images and narratives, our idea is to picture these people and, at the same time, to share something of the story of their lives. Seeing where and how they work and live, meeting their family and friends, and learning something of both their lives to date and their hopes for the future, we would honour each person's dignity. The images could be shared and the stories told in a book or documentary film, or both.

Figure 9 Bringing our humanity to life

Who would do this work? While we can imagine teaming up with a videographer to travel the world in search of these people and their stories, we can also imagine enlisting business students to help. Such an effort would be fully consistent with the United Nations' aspiration for business education. Recall that they launched their Principles for Responsible Management Education (PRME) initiative in 2007. The Appendix captures the six principles that they would like to see every business school embrace. Done well, a business school could send its students the world over to collect the images and stories. Such an effort would absolutely honour each of the PRME's six principles (in the areas of purpose, values, method, research, partnership and dialogue).

This work might even add life to the PRME initiative. While the PRME webpage today counts more than 650 business schools in over 80 counties as signatories, denominators matter here too (PRME, 2016). The AACSB (2015) counted 16,484 degree granting business schools in 2015. While 650 is a large number, these signatories comprise just 3.9% of the world's business schools. We also noticed that just 2 of the top 20 business schools in the USA are signatories—Cornell University and University of California, Berkeley.[14] Enlist some of the world's "top" business schools in this effort, and perhaps others will follow. Once the humanity of one product's value chain has been so revealed (and we learn how to efficiently and effectively complete this kind of project), it may be that students in business schools the world over could pick their favourite product and document the humanity in that sphere of business activity.[15] Build an accessible library of such efforts and we just might inspire the world to act. The good news is that done at scale, this work ensures that

---

14 Average the *Business Week* MBA rankings for programmes in the USA between 1988 and 2015, rank order the results, and the following schools emerge as the top 20 programmes: Northwestern (Kellogg), Pennsylvania (Wharton), Harvard, Chicago (Booth), Michigan (Ross), Stanford, Columbia, Duke (Fuqua), MIT (Sloan), Dartmouth (Tuck), Virginia (Darden), Cornell (Johnson), UCLA (Anderson), UC Berkeley (Haas), Carnegie-Mellon (Tepper), North Carolina (Kenan-Flagler), NYU (Stern) and Indiana (Kelley), Yale, and Texas (McCombs). No "top 10" school is a signatory.

15 Such an effort would be fully consistent with the many efforts in recent years to bring business students out of the classroom and into the world. Godfrey (1999) and Godfrey *et al.* (2005), for example, have encouraged us for years to enable our students to serve the world as they complete their studies, both for the world's benefit and for their own development (see Yorio and Ye (2012) for a look at how students benefit from such work). The growing prevalence of study abroad programs (see NAFSA and the commitment of its 3,500 member institutions worldwide to international education: http://www.nafsa. org/About_Us/About_NAFSA/) and the Forum on Education Abroad with its nearly 800 member institutions, also dedicated to international education (https://forumea.org/), as well as action-based learning (ABL) programmes (see the University of Michigan's Ross School of Business's now 25-year commitment to ABL (http://michiganross.umich. edu/our-community/companies/map) and the University of Leeds' "Leeds for Life" programme that enables their students to make a difference in their local community (https:// leedsforlife.leeds.ac.uk/) suggest that the time may be ripe for such an initiative.

our future business leaders will know in their bones that their work can—and should—serve humanity.[16]

Final thoughts

We began by observing that Pope Francis appeals to the better nature of our angels and that the United Nations offers business a path ahead to help make the world a better place. We are well aware that these efforts can be seen as limited. After all, the Pope "only" offered us a set of aspirational reflections and an appeal. One might argue that values, no matter how laudatory, must be brought to life with a complementary system of accountability and control. The United Nations offered a path in that direction but to be sure, it is a rocky one. Holding aside questions about its limited embrace, we recognize that the Global Compact is largely an unenforceable voluntary code of conduct. Such codes can be used to forestall demanding government regulations, regulations that would require exacting disclosure, careful monitoring and tough sanctions for non-compliance (King and Lennox, 2000; Delmas and Montes-Sancho, 2010). Such codes can also be adopted to fuel a corporate communication strategy that misleads a firm's stakeholders about its operations (Lyon and Montgomery, 2015). Some might argue that the entire enterprise is ill-conceived. Soederberg (2007) and Sethi and Schepers (2014), for example, are vocal critics. They are not shy:

> ... the GC acts to legitimize and normalize the expropriation of labour, while seeking to neutralize and depoliticize struggle tied to the deepening and widening forms of economic exploitation in the global South by powerful TNCs and their global supply chains (see Taylor, 2007) (Soederberg, 2007, p. 510).

> ... the UNGC has projected itself as the empyrean of high moral and humanistic values, while in practice, it has struggled in the trenches with lowly mortals, not to save them, but for their patronage to save itself. In this position, the UNGC is incapable of either redeeming itself or making discernible progress in its mission. Perhaps the most honorable approach would be for the UNGC to admit its failure and dissolve itself (Sethi and Schepers, 2014, p. 207).

Aware of these criticisms, we still walk away impressed by the United Nations and the Vatican's work. We are inspired by their high aspirations. After all, it is one thing to identify the world's problems, it is an entirely different matter to step up and try to do something about them. We admire their gumption. Limitations and troubles notwithstanding, no situation is irredeemable. If well-meaning people take well-meaning criticism to heart, wrongs can be righted.

---

16 Once fully launched, we can imagine that this kind of project could also be crowdsourced. In time, we envision a structured and searchable web platform that allows people around the world to upload their own photos and videos and in doing so, tell their own stories.

As we work to better the Global Compact, for example, we need to remember that we are dealing with global problems. We may long for demanding government regulations, exacting disclosure requirements, careful monitoring and tough sanctions for non-compliance, but we do not have a world government capable of bringing such a dream to life. As constituted, the United Nations certainly cannot do that today. To be sure, nation-states can take up the challenge but absent harmonization, the door is always open to opportunities for regulatory arbitrage (see Houston *et al.*, 2012). And so, even as we move forward to right wrongs and better govern our world, we need to recognize that at base, our values will inspire any global governance regime we imagine. Values matter. They matter too because they inspire and enable individuals and firms' more local actions, actions that in time may cohere and scale to change the world (Weick, 1984). Just as lives are lived one at a time, the world changes one act at a time. Every act of conscience matters.

Perhaps it is fair to say that, most fundamentally, the United Nations has been trying to change our minds about business. They are looking to move business leaders to work for human rights and against labour abuses, for the environment and against corruption. Pope Francis, on the other hand, is trying to touch souls, the innermost aspect of humankind, the spiritual principle that defines what it means to be a person (Catholic Church, 1995, p. 363). Indeed, he ends his encyclical by asking God to "Bring healing to our lives, that we may protect the world and not prey on it, that we may sow beauty, not pollution and destruction" (LS, 246). And with all modesty, we are trying to stir hearts with our proposal here. If we can only find a way for us to see and, yes, even feel each other's' dignity, then we might actually treat each other, and our home, the planet itself, with deserved respect. Compassion fade and compassion fatigue are real. Nevertheless, with an open mind, a generous heart and a compassionate soul, we just might temper our self-serving inclinations and make the world a better place.

References

AACSB (2015). *Business School Data Guide*. Retrieved from: http://www.aacsb.edu/~/media/AACSB/Publications/data-trends-booklet/2015.ashx

Adler, P.S., Forbes, L.C., & Wilmott, H. (2007). Critical management studies. *Academy of Management Annals*, 1, 119-179.

Bamberger, B., & Davidson, C.N. (1998). *Closing: The Life and Death of an American Factory*. New York: W.W. Norton & Company.

Blinder, A.S. (2006). Offshoring: The next industrial revolution? *Foreign Affairs*, 85, 113-128.

Blinder, A.S., & Krueger, A.B. (2013). Alternative measures of offshorability: A survey approach. *Journal of Labor Economics*, 31(2), S97-S128.

Brown, S.J., & Warner, J.B. (1985). Using daily stock returns: The case of event studies. *Journal of Financial Economics*, 14, 3-21.

Catholic Church (1995). *Catechism of the Catholic Church* (2nd ed.). New York: Doubleday.

Delmas, M.A., & Montes-Sancho, M.J. (2010). Voluntary agreements to improve environmental quality: Symbolic and substantive cooperation. *Strategic Management Journal*, 31, 575-601.

Donaldson, T., & Walsh, J. P. (2015). Toward a theory of business. *Research in Organizational Behavior*, 35, 181-207.

Dun & Bradstreet (2015). *DNBi International Report Enhancements & Special Offers*: Retrieved from: http://www.dnb.com/lc/credit-education/enhanced-dnbi-for-better-global-market-intelligence.html#.VZAqoflViko

Figley, C.R. (1995). *Compassion Fatigue: Coping with Secondary Traumatic Stress Disorder in those who Treat the Traumatized*. New York: Brunner/Mazel.

Francis I (2015). *Encyclical letter "Laudato Si": On Care for Our Common Home*. Vatican City: Vatican Press. Retrieved from: http://w2.vatican.va/content/francesco/en/encyclicals/documents/papa-francesco_20150524_enciclica-laudato-si.html

Francis I (2016). *Amoris Laetitia*. Retrieved from: https://w2.vatican.va/content/dam/francesco/pdf/apost_exhortations/documents/papa-francesco_esortazione-ap_20160319_amoris-laetitia_en.pdf

Godfrey, P.C. (1999). Service-learning and management education: A call to action. *Journal of Management Inquiry*, 8(4), 363-378.

Godfrey, P.C., Illes, L.M., & Berry, G.R. (2005). Creating breadth in business education through service learning. *Academy of Management Learning and Education*, 4(3), 309-323.

Houston, J.F., Lin, C., & Ma, Y. (2012). Regulatory arbitrage and international bank flows. *Journal of Finance*, 67(5), 1845-1895.

Janney, J.J., Dess, G., & Forlani, V. (2009). Glass houses? Market reactions to firms joining the UN Global Compact. *Journal of Business Ethics*, 90(3), 407-423.

Kania, J., & Kramer, M. (2011). Collective impact. *Stanford Social Innovation Review*, 9, 36-41.

Kay, K. (2016, June 20). Five reasons Brexit could signal Trump winning the White House. *BBC News*. Retrieved from: http://www.bbc.com/news/election-us-2016-36564808

Kell, G., Kingo, L., & Reynolds, F. (2015, August 7). Open Letter to His Holiness Pope Francis from the United Nations Global Compact Responding to Laudato Si. Retrieved from: https://www.unglobalcompact.org/docs/issues_doc/Environment/Laudato_Si_Open_Letter_UN_Global_Compact.pdf

King, A.A., & Lennox, M.J. (2000). Industry self-regulation without sanctions: The chemical industry's responsible care program. *Academy of Management Journal*, 43(4), 698-716.

London, T. (2016). *The Base of the Pyramid Promise*. Stanford, CA: Stanford University Press.

Lyon, T.P, & Montgomery, A.W. (2015). The means and ends of greenwash. *Organization & Environment*, 28(2), 223-249.

Margolis, J.D., & Walsh, J.P. (2003). Misery loves companies: Rethinking social initiatives by business. *Administrative Science Quarterly*, 48, 265-305.

Pontifical Council for Justice and Peace (2015, August 13). Open Letter to His Holiness Pope Francis from the United Nations Global Compact Responding to Laudato Si. Retrieved from: http://www.iustitiaetpax.va/content/giustiziaepace/en/speciale-laudato-si/approfondimenti/open-letter-to-his-holiness-pope-francis-from-the-united-nations.html

Porter, M.E., & Kramer, M.R. (2011). Creating shared value. *Harvard Business Review*, 89 (1/2), 62-77.

Porter, M.E., & Stern, S. (2015). *Social Progress Index 2015*. Retrieved from: http://www.socialprogressimperative.org/publications

PRME (2016). Signatories. Retrieved from: http://www.unprme.org/participants/index.php

Reiser, D.B. (2011). Benefit corporations: A sustainable form of organization? *Wake Forest Law Review*, 46, 591-625.

Schlesinger, Jr, A.M. (1986). *The Cycles of American History*. Boston, MA: Houghton Mifflin Company.

Schlesinger, A.M. (1949). *Paths to the Present*. New York: The Macmillan Company.

Sethi, S.P., & Schepers, D.H. (2014). United Nations Global Compact: The promise–performance gap. *Journal of Business Ethics*, 122(2), 193-208.

Slovic, P. (2007). "If I look at the mass, I will never act": Psychic numbing and genocide. *Judgment and Decision Making*, 2(2), 79-95.

Slovic, S., & Slovic, P. (2015). Postscript. In S. Slovic & P. Slovic (Eds.), *Numbers and Nerves: Information, Emotion, and Meaning in a World of Data* (pp. 217-220). Corvallis, OR: Oregon State University Press.

Slovic, P., & Västfjäll, D. (2015). The more who die, the less we care: Psychic numbing and genocide. In S. Slovic & P. Slovic (Eds.), *Numbers and Nerves: Information, Emotion, and Meaning in a World of Data* (pp. 27-41). Corvallis, OR: Oregon State University Press.

Smolan, R., & Cohen, D.E. (1986). *A Day in the Life of America*. New York: Collins Publishers.

Soederberg, S. (2007). Taming corporations or buttressing market-led development? A critical assessment of the Global Compact. *Globalizations*, 4(4), 500-513.

Taylor, M. (2007). Rethinking the global production of uneven development. *Globalizations*, 4(4), 529-542.

Turk, S. (2015, November). *IBISWorld Industry Report OD6098 The Retail Market for Coffee*. Retrieved from: www.ibisworld.com

United Nations (2015). *The Millennium Development Goals Report*. Retrieved from: http://www.un.org/millenniumgoals/2015_MDG_Report/pdf/MDG%202015%20rev%20(July%201).pdf

Valkila, J., Haaparanta, P., & Niemi, N. (2010). Empowering coffee traders? The coffee value chain from Nicaraguan Fair Trade farmers to Finnish consumers. *Journal of Business Ethics*, 97, 257-270.

Weick, K.E. (1984). Small wins: Redefining the scale of social problems. *American Psychologist*, 39(1), 40-49.

Wilson, E.O. (2014). *The Meaning of Human Existence*. New York: Liveright Publishing Corporation.

Yorio, P.L., & Ye, F. (2012). A meta-analysis on the effects of service-learning on the social, personal, and cognitive outcomes of learning. *Academy of Management Learning and Education*, 11(1), 9-27.

Appendix: United Nations Principles for Responsible Management Education

Principle 1 | Purpose: We will develop the capabilities of students to be future generators of sustainable value for business and society at large and to work for an inclusive and sustainable global economy.

Principle 2 | Values: We will incorporate into our academic activities and curricula the values of global social responsibility as portrayed in international initiatives such as the United Nations Global Compact.

Principle 3 | Method: We will create educational frameworks, materials, processes and environments that enable effective learning experiences for responsible leadership.

Principle 4 | Research: We will engage in conceptual and empirical research that advances our understanding about the role, dynamics, and impact of corporations in the creation of sustainable social, environmental and economic value.

Principle 5 | Partnership: We will interact with managers of business corporations to extend our knowledge of their challenges in meeting social and environmental responsibilities and to explore jointly effective approaches to meeting these challenges.

Principle 6 | Dialogue: We will facilitate and support dialog and debate among educators, students, business, government, consumers, media, civil society organisations and other interested groups and stakeholders on critical issues related to global social responsibility and sustainability.

About the *Journal of Corporate Citizenship*

THE JOURNAL OF CORPORATE CITIZENSHIP (*JCC*) is a multidisciplinary peer-reviewed journal that focuses on integrating theory about corporate citizenship with management practice. It provides a forum in which the tensions and practical realities of making corporate citizenship real can be addressed in a reader-friendly, yet conceptually and empirically rigorous format.

JCC aims to publish *the best ideas integrating the theory and practice of corporate citizenship in a format that is readable, accessible, engaging, interesting and useful* for readers in its already wide audience in business, consultancy, government, NGOs and academia. It encourages practical, theoretically sound, and (when relevant) empirically rigorous manuscripts that address real-world implications of corporate citizenship in global and local contexts. Topics related to corporate citizenship can include (but are not limited to): corporate responsibility, stakeholder relationships, public policy, sustainability and environment, human and labour rights/ issues, governance, accountability and transparency, globalization, small and medium-sized enterprises (SMEs) as well as multinational firms, ethics, measurement, and specific issues related to corporate citizenship, such as diversity, poverty, education, information, trust, supply chain management, and problematic or constructive corporate/human behaviours and practices.

In addition to articles linking the theory and practice of corporate citizenship, *JCC* also encourages Innovative or creative submissions (for peer review). Innovative submissions can highlight issues of corporate citizenship from a critical perspective, enhance practical or conceptual understanding of corporate citizenship, or provide new insights or alternative perspectives on the realities of corporate citizenship in today's world. Innovative submissions might include: critical perspectives and controversies, photography, essays, poetry, drama, reflections, and other innovations that help bring corporate citizenship to life for management practitioners and academics alike.

JCC welcomes contributions from researchers and practitioners involved in any of the areas mentioned above. Manuscripts should be written so that they are comprehensible to an intelligent reader, avoiding jargon, formulas and extensive methodological treatises wherever possible. They should use examples and illustrations to highlight the ideas, concepts and practical implications of the ideas being presented. Theory is important and necessary; but theory—with the empirical research and conceptual work that supports theory— needs to be balanced by integration into practices to stand the tests of time and usefulness. *JCC* aims to be the premier journal to publish articles on corporate citizenship that accomplish this integration of theory and practice. We want the journal to be read as much by executives leading corporate citizenship as it is by academics seeking sound research and scholarship.

JCC appears quarterly and includes peer-reviewed papers by leading writers, with occasional reviews, case studies and think-pieces. A key feature is the "Turning Points" section. Turning Points are commentaries, controversies, new ideas, essays and insights that aim to be provocative and engaging, raise the important issues of the day and provide observations on what is too new yet to be the subject of empirical and theoretical studies. *JCC* continues to produce occasional issues dedicated to a single theme. These have included "Story Telling: Beyond the Academic Article—Using Fiction, Art and Literary Techniques to Communicate", "Sustainable Luxury", "Business–NGO Partnerships", "Creating Global Citizens and Responsible Leadership", "Responsible Investment in Emerging Markets", "The Positive Psychology of Sustainable Enterprise", "Textiles, Fashion and Sustainability", "Designing Management Education", "Managing by Design" and "Innovative Stakeholder Engagement".

EDITORS

General Editor:

Dr David F. Murphy, Institute for Leadership and Sustainability (IFLAS), University of Cumbria, UK; email: david.murphy@greenleaf-publishing.com

Regional Editor:

North American Editor: Sandra Waddock, Galligan Chair of Strategy, Carroll School Scholar of Corporate Responsibility, and Professor of Management, Carroll School of Management, Boston College. Senior Research Fellow, Center for Corporate Citizenship, Chestnut Hill, MA 02467 USA; tel: +1 617 552 0477; fax: +1 617 552 0433; email: waddock@bc.edu

Notes for Contributors

SUBMISSIONS

All content should be submitted via online submission. For more information see the journal homepage at www.greenleaf-publishing.com/journals/journal-of-corporate-citizenship.

The form gives prompts for the required information and asks authors to submit the full text of the paper, including the title, author name and author affiliation, as a Word attachment. **Abstract and keywords will be completed via the online submission and are not necessary on the attachment.**

As part of the online submission authors will be asked to tick a box to state they have read and adhere to the Greenleaf–GSE Copyright Guidelines and have permission to publish the paper, including all figures, images, etc. which have been taken from other sources. It is the author's responsibility to ensure this is correct.

In order to be able to distribute papers published in Greenleaf journals, we need signed transfer of copyright from the authors. We are committed to a liberal and fair approach to copyright and accessibility, and do not restrict authors' rights to reuse their own work for personal use or in an institutional repository.

A brief autobiographical note should be supplied at the end of the paper including:

- Full name
- Affiliation
- Email address
- Full international contact details

Please supply (via online submission) an **abstract outlining the title, purpose, methodology and main findings**. It's worth considering that, as your paper will be located and read online, the quality of your abstract will determine whether readers go on to access your full paper. We recommend you place particular focus on the impact of your research on further research, practice or society. What does your paper contribute?

In addition, please provide up to **six descriptive keywords**.

Please address all new manuscripts via the online submission system to the General Editor, David F. Murphy.

FORMATTING YOUR PAPER

Headings should be short and in bold text, with a clear and consistent hierarchy.

Please identify **Notes or Endnotes** with consecutive numbers, enclosed in square brackets and listed at the end of the article.

Figures and other images should be submitted as .jpeg (.jpg) or .tif files and be of a high quality. Please number consecutively with Arabic numerals and mark clearly within the body of the text where they should be placed.

If images are not the original work of the author, it is the author's responsibility to obtain written consent from the copyright holder to them being used. Authors will be asked to confirm this is the case by ticking the box on the online submission to say they have read and understood the Greenleaf–GSE copyright policy. Images which are neither the authors' own work, nor are accompanied by such permission will not be published.

Tables should be included as part of the manuscript, with relevant captions.

Supplementary data can be appended to the article, using the form and should follow the same formatting rules as the main text

References to other publications should be complete and in Harvard style, e.g. (Jones, 2011) for one author, (Jones and Smith, 2011) for two authors and (Jones *et al.*, 2011) for more than two authors. A full reference list should appear at the end of the paper

- For **books**: Surname, Initials (year). *Title of Book*, Place of publication: Publisher.
  e.g. Author, J. (2011). *This is my book*, New York, NY: Publisher.
- For **book chapters**: Surname, Initials (year). Chapter title. In Editor's Initials, Editor's Surname (Ed.), *Title of Book* (pp. X-Y). Place of publication: Publisher.
- For **journals**: Surname, Initials (year). Title of article. *Title of Journal*, volume (number), pages.
- For **conference proceedings**: Surname, Initials (year). Title of paper. In Editor's Initials, Editor's Surname (Ed.), *Title of published proceeding which may include place and date(s) held* (pp. X-Y). Place of publication: Publisher.
- For **newspaper articles**: Surname, Initials (year, month date) (if an author is named). Article title. *Newspaper*, pages.
- For **images**:
  Where image is from a printed source—as for books but with the page number on which the image appears.
  Where image is from an online source—Surname, Initials (year), Title. Retrieved from: URL of website.
  Other images—Surname, Initials (year), Title, Name of owner (person or institution) and location for viewing.
- For **web pages**: Surname, Initials (year). *Title of web page*. Retrieved from: URL of website.

▶ **To discuss ideas for contributions**, please contact the General Editor: Dr David F. Murphy; email: david.murphy@greenleaf-publishing.com.

Journal of Corporate Citizenship

Call for Papers

Special Issue: 'Leading Wellbeing in Rural Contexts'

What are the unique challenges of rurality for communities and businesses and how can we address them?

Worldwide, 46% of the population is classified as rural, although there is considerable variation across developing and developed countries. There are related demographical challenges which are impacted by the availability of, and access to, services.

There is an emerging understanding of the key differences between rural and urban services, the importance of context, place and community, and the need to harness input from the private, voluntary and third sectors more effectively. It may be that it is necessary to discover and develop a way to deliver rural services differently, recognising limitations of the geopolitical context and supporting people to create a new paradigm that is community based, rather than service based.

Contributions

We are open to a wide range of contributors. We encourage submissions from academics as well as practitioners working in the public, private and the voluntary sectors from diverse geographical, cultural and political contexts.

Possible research explorations may include but are not restricted to:

- Analysis of issues and associated solutions with regards to rural services, infrastructure and related technological challenges
- Understanding the role of different sectors and cross-sector collaboration in the design and delivery of rural services and infrastructure
- Reviewing workforce development issues and solutions
- Case studies of innovative rural service design and delivery

The JCC also encourages innovative or creative submissions, including critical perspectives and controversies, photography, essays, poetry and other innovations that help bring corporate citizenship to life for management practitioners and academics.

Schedule

Authors should send an abstract of approximately 300 words to: **alison.marshall@cumbria.ac.uk** no later than 31 January 2017. For full details of this special issue and the submission schedule, please visit **www.greenleaf-publishing.com/journals/journal-of-corporate-citizenship** and click on the 'Calls for Papers' tab.

Introducing our eCollections on Sustainability and Responsible Leadership